On the Edge of Disaster

Youth in the Juvenile Court System

On the Edge of Disaster

Youth in the Juvenile Court System

BY DONNA LANGE

MASON CREST PUBLISHERS

The author would like to thank the following for their contributions to this book: Ann Bronson, Elizabeth Bronson, Investigator Vincent A. Cordi, Tina Gilmore, Attorney Lars Mead, Neil Payne, Carol Pike, and members of the Vestal Police Department, Vestal, New York. Special thanks go to the author's husband, Gary; children: Jonathan, Stephanie, and Christine.

Mason Crest Publishers
370 Reed Road, Broomall, Pennsylvania 19008
(866) MCP-BOOK (toll free)
www.masoncrest.com

First edition, 2004
13 12 11 10 09 08 07 06 05 04   10 9 8 7 6 5 4 3 2

Library of Congress Cataloging-in-Publication Data
Lange, Donna.
On the edge of disaster: youth in the juvenile court system / by Donna Lange.
v.cm.—(Youth with special needs)
Includes bibliographic references and index.
Contents:Trouble—Caught—Mistakes—Youth court—Steps toward serenity—Learning more—Living with the consequences—Heading toward the future.
1.Juvenile deliquency—United States—Juvenile literature. 2.Juvenile justice, Administration of—United States—Juvenile literature. [1. Juvenile deliquency. 2. Justice, Administration of.] I. Title. II. Series
HV9104.L325 2004
364.36'0973—dc22.   2003018643

ISBN 1-59084-741-5
1-59084-727-X (series)

Design by Harding House Publishing Service, Inc.
Composition by Bytheway Publishing Services, Binghamton, New York.
Cover art by Keith Rosko.
Cover design by Benjamin Stewart.
Produced by Harding House Publishing Service, Vestal, New York.
Printed in the Hashemite Kingdom of Jordan.

The juvenile justice system process is different for the United States and Canada, and within each nation, it is often different for each state or province and may even vary between communities within a state or province. Therefore, all descriptions are general, unless noted otherwise. The information contained in this book is for informational purposes only. Please seek legal advice from an attorney.

Picture credits: Artville: pp. 49, 100. Benjamin Stewart: pp. 33, 34, 35, 38, 80, 90, 92, 102, 103, 116, 117, 118. Corbis: pp. 17, 20, 32, 37, 47, 48, 52, 61, 62, 63, 65, 66, 76, 77, 78, 89, 113, 114, 119. PhotoDisc: pp. 18, 51, 75, 79, 115; the individuals in these images are models, and the images are for illustrative purposes only.

CONTENTS

A child with special needs is not defined by his disability.
It is just one part of who he is.

INTRODUCTION

Each child is unique and wonderful. And some children have differences we call special needs. Special needs can mean many things. Sometimes children will learn differently, or hear with an aid, or read with Braille. A young person may have a hard time communicating or paying attention. A child can be born with a special need, or acquire it by an accident or through a health condition. Sometimes a child will be developing in a typical manner and then become delayed in that development. But whatever problems a child may have with her learning, emotions, behavior, or physical body, she is always a person first. She is not defined by her disability; instead, the disability is just one part of who she is.

Inclusion means that young people with and without special needs are together in the same settings. They learn together in school; they play together in their communities; they all have the same opportunities to belong. Children learn so much from each other. A child with a hearing impairment, for example, can teach another child a new way to communicate using sign language. Someone else who has a physical disability affecting his legs can show his friends how to play wheelchair basketball. Children with and without special needs can teach each other how to appreciate and celebrate their differences. They can also help each other discover how people are more alike than they are different. Understanding and appreciating how we all have similar needs helps us learn empathy and sensitivity.

In this series, you will read about young people with special needs from the unique perspectives of children and adolescents who are experiencing the disability firsthand. Of course, not all children with a particular disability are the same as the characters in the stories. But the stories demonstrate at an emotional level how a special need impacts a child, his family, and his friends. The factual material in each chapter will expand your horizons by adding to your knowledge about a particular disability. The series as a whole will help you understand differences better and appreciate how they make us all stronger and better.

—*Cindy Croft*
Educational Consultant

YOUTH WITH SPECIAL NEEDS provides a unique forum for demystifying a wide variety of childhood medical and developmental disabilities. Written to captivate an adolescent audience, the books bring to life the challenges and triumphs experienced by children with common chronic conditions such as hearing loss, mental retardation, physical differences, and speech difficulties. The topics are addressed frankly through a blend of fiction and fact. Students and teachers alike can move beyond the information provided by accessing the resources offered at the end of each text.

This series is particularly important today as the number of children with special needs is on the rise. Over the last two decades, advances in pediatric medical techniques have allowed children who have chronic illnesses and disabilities to live longer, more functional lives. As a result, these children represent an increasingly visible part of North American population in all aspects of daily life. Students are exposed to peers with special needs in their classrooms, through extracurricular activities, and in the community. Often, young people have misperceptions and unanswered questions about a child's disabilities—and more important, his or her *abilities*. Many times, there is no vehicle for talking about these complex issues in a comfortable manner.

This series provides basic information that will leave readers with a deeper understanding of each condition, along with an awareness of some of the associated emotional impacts on affected children, their families, and their peers. It will also encourage further conversation about these issues. Most important, the series promotes a greater comfort for its readers as they live, play, and work side by side with these individuals who have medical and developmental differences—youth with special needs.

—Dr. Lisa Albers, Dr. Carolyn Bridgemohan, Dr. Laurie Glader
Medical Consultants

Crime is contagious.
—Louis D. Brandeis, Supreme Court Justice

1

TROUBLE

Just like every other Friday evening, I ate dinner alone. When the phone rang, I don't know why I bothered to answer—I knew it was Jeremy, because he called me every other Friday night. But since I had no other plans, I picked up the phone.

"Hey, Zeek, wanna shoot hoops?" Jeremy asked.

Jeremy wasn't good at basketball, but I didn't have anything else to do that night. "Sure," I said.

"I'll be right over." He hung up without even saying good-bye.

Although I had gone to this high school for most of my freshman year, I still didn't feel accepted. I thought this place would be different. I remember the day we moved here; I hoped my life would be better, that it would be easier for me to make friends. But I soon learned that even though other minority families lived in the area, I was the only multiracial kid in the neighborhood. Both at school and in the neighborhood, kids would say hi to me, but Jeremy was the only one that ever asked to do anything with me.

I rinsed the dishes and set them in the drainer. I sure didn't want Dad having another reason to yell when he got home. He always seemed to yell the most on Friday nights.

Jeremy rang the doorbell. I opened the door and he walked into the living room, bouncing a basketball.

"Hey, Zeek, you alone?"

"Yeah, Mom took Carlos and Jadira to stay with my grandparents, and then she went to finish her double shift."

"Wanna play 'hide-n-drink'?" Jeremy grinned.

"Okay. Dad won't be home from work for a few more hours. He'll never know."

I poured a small glass of water, and then we walked to the shed at the end of the driveway. Inside the shed, I reached behind a red toolbox and pulled out a bottle of vodka.

Jeremy laughed. "I can't believe your old man still hides it in here."

"Yeah. I guess he figures Mom won't know since she can't smell it on his breath."

We took turns chugging the vodka. After a few swigs, I poured a little water in the bottle to make it look like no one had touched it. With Jeremy following me, I closed the shed, put the empty glass back on the kitchen counter, and we headed down the street. If we talked, I don't remember what we said. After a couple blocks, we walked around the side of the school, toward the basketball court.

"Zeek, I got something to show you. You aren't gonna believe it!" Jeremy pointed. "It's over there."

We walked to the edge of the school property. Jeremy crawled behind some bushes and held up a full-size skeleton.

"I took it from a science room earlier today. I figure I can pull a great prank on someone. Who should I scare?"

"I don't know," I said slowly.

I looked at the skeleton while Jeremy talked about what he could do with it. Finally, he placed the skeleton on the ground and we walked to the basketball court.

A few minutes later, Jeremy stopped shooting hoops. "See that little window in the door of the school?"

"Yeah," I said.

"Let's have a contest, see who can break it first." He dropped the basketball.

I know it was a bad choice, but I agreed. We each picked up a rock and threw it at the window. We weren't far from the building because even though the window was small, both of our rocks hit the window—almost at the same time. The glass shattered.

"Hey, you!" a janitor shouted through a classroom window.

"Jeremy, someone saw us."

Jeremy laughed. "What's he gonna do, hit us with a mop?"

"Joe, there's a couple kids outside throwing rocks!" the janitor yelled to someone.

"But there's more than one person in there," I said.

"So there're two janitors." Jeremy started running. "Come on," he said over his shoulder, "they'll never catch us."

I picked up the basketball and headed to the street, but Jeremy said he didn't want to leave the skeleton. So I turned around and went with him behind the bushes. All of a sudden, I heard a deep male voice.

"Boys, come on out," a man said.

I froze.

"I said to come out," the man said louder. "Put your hands over your heads and kneel on the ground."

Jeremy and I crawled out from behind the bushes, knelt on the ground, and lifted our hands. Two police officers towered over us. One officer told me to stand up, and then he searched me while the other office did the same to Jeremy. Then the older officer told us to turn around.

"What do we have here, another friend?" The younger officer pointed to the skeleton.

"Looks like he could use something to eat." The older officer laughed.

"What's your name?" the younger officer asked.

"Jeremy Hughes."

"Zeek Martinez," I said.

"Zeek, is that your real name?" the younger officer asked me.

"It's short for Ezekiel," I muttered.

"Ezekiel. Haven't heard that name in awhile."

"I was named after my grandfather," I said.

"Nothing wrong with a grandfather's name, Ezekiel," the older officer said. "Boys, you've just won yourselves a ride to the station."

I felt like I was in a cloud. I could hear an officer talking with Jeremy, but I didn't pay attention to them. I don't even know what happened to the skeleton. I just looked at the ground as an officer clasped the cold steel handcuffs around my wrists and walked me to the police car.

HISTORY OF AMERICA'S JUVENILE JUSTICE

America's juvenile justice system came from the English. They believed that at age seven, children were able to tell the difference between right and wrong. If it could be shown that children between ages eight and fourteen were intelligent enough to understand the nature and consequences of what they had done, these children could be held responsible for criminal acts. They could be subjected to the same type of trial and sentence as adults.

In 1684, a girl named Jane Owen was indicted for stealing a silver mustard pot and three silver spoons. She was found guilty and was sentenced "to be burnt in the hand."

A New Parent

Parens patriae is a Latin phrase used when the government acts as the guardian to protect the interests of children who cannot take care of themselves; it is sometimes referred to as "the state acting in the best interest of the child."

The concept of the state as parent was introduced in America in 1636 when a young boy of Plymouth Colony was given to a widow to keep as a foster child. But the concept had actually begun earlier, in England, during the late fourteenth and early fifteenth centuries, when the King's Court of Chancery had the power of guardianship over abandoned or neglected children.

Juvenile Court Act

On July 1, 1899, the Juvenile Court Act became law in the state of Illinois. Under this new law, the **juvenile court** had power over the treatment and control of dependent, neglected, and delinquent children. The court became responsible for the child. This court could place children with individuals or in institutions that would take the place of unsuit-able family homes. The child who had offended the law ceased to be a criminal and was now considered a child who needed care, protection, and discipline. At this point in time, the emphasis was on treatment rather than on punish-ment.

First Juvenile Court

Jane Addams was one of the most outstanding citizens who contributed to improving conditions for juvenile offenders. In 1899, Jane Addams and other women founded Hull House, located in Chicago's ghetto. The women wanted to understand the causes of delinquency. They struggled to offer children an opportunity to heal and to find a way for young people to get out of a life in crime. They were filled with optimism. They said the juvenile court would act in every instance exactly as a "kind and just parent" would act.

A Role Model

The Juvenile Court of Cook County, Illinois, was imitated throughout the United States. Eventually, various types of ju-venile courts reached all states, with the last state enacting the necessary legislation in 1945.

Although the introduction of juvenile courts seemed a great step forward from courts where children were taken into **custody**. The "kindly parent, the state" is an expression that is sometimes used sarcastically.

WHO IS A JUVENILE?

It depends on your birthday. By law, you are a juvenile until the day after your state says that you are an adult—unless a court rules differently.

The scales represent the court system, where a person's offenses are weighed and measured.

When a young person gets in trouble with the law, he will be tried in a special court system designed specifically for juveniles.

At what age does juvenile status for a ***juvenile delinquent*** terminate?

Age	States
16	Connecticut, New York, North Carolina, Vermont
17	Georgia, Illinois, Louisiana, Massachusetts, Missouri, South Carolina, Texas
18	Alabama, Alaska, Arizona, Arkansas, California, Colorado, Delaware, District of Columbia, Florida, Hawaii, Idaho, Indiana, Iowa, Kansas, Kentucky, Maine, Maryland, Michigan, Minnesota, Mississippi, Montana, Nebraska, Nevada, New Hampshire, New Jersey, New Mexico, North Dakota, Ohio, Oklahoma, Oregon, Pennsylvania, Rhode Island, South Dakota, Tennessee, Utah, Virginia, Washington, West Virginia, Wisconsin
19	Wyoming

AGES OF JUVENILES IN THE SYSTEM

Throughout the country, jurisdictions have adopted laws that limit or eliminate juvenile court jurisdiction. In Georgia, juveniles fourteen years old and older who commit violent ***crimes*** are now automatically tried as adults. The law in Pennsylvania applies to juveniles fifteen years and older. States, including Illinois, Arizona, and Colorado, either have new laws in place or proposed for the near future.

In 1995, Hawaii was the only state still treating all youth under sixteen as juveniles in all cases.

In California, legislation makes it harder to sentence someone back into the juvenile system after he has been transferred to adult court. It was never easy, but now it's almost impossible.

DID YOU KNOW?

- In 1996, law enforcement agencies made 723,000 arrests of females below the age of 18.
- In 2000, law enforcement agencies made 655,700 arrests of females below the age of 18.

HOW DO WE KNOW HOW MANY JUVENILES ARE COMMITTING CRIMES?

The Uniform Crime Reporting (UCR) Program was started in 1929 by the International Association of Chiefs of Police in order to supply reliable crime statistics for the United States. The UCR gives Americans statistics about who is committing crimes and where.

- Who prepares this report?
  The FBI.
- What is the title of the report?
  Crime in the United States.
- When is the report prepared?
  Every year.
- Where does the FBI get the information?
  More than 17,000 local law enforcement agencies
  throughout the country.
- How is the report compiled?
  The report summarizes crimes known to the police
  and arrests made during the reporting calendar year.
- Why is the report compiled?
  This information is used to describe the amount and
  character of crimes, including juvenile crimes. It helps
  law enforcement agencies see what is working—and
  what isn't.
  (Adapted from http://ojjdp.ncjrs.org/jjbulletin/
  jjbul_1197/jjb1197.html#one)

In Canada, the Canadian Centre for Justice Statistics collects
and publishes the same sort of statistics.

A Message from the Office of Juvenile Justice and Delinquency Prevention

Juvenile Arrests 2000 summarizes the information presented
in the FBI report *Crime in the United States 2000*, showing:

- Juvenile violent crime arrests have declined for the
  sixth straight year.
- In 2000, the juvenile arrest rate for violent crime was
  41 percent below its peak in 1994. This is the lowest
  level in fourteen years.
- The juvenile arrest rate for murder dropped 74 percent

from its peak in 1993. This is its lowest level since the 1960s.

(Adapted from www.ncjrs.org/html/ojjdp/ jjbul2002_11_1/contents.html)

JUVENILE CRIME IN CANADA

In 1994, the percentage of U.S. juveniles arrested for violent crimes was twice as high as the Canadian rate.

Arrests per 100,000 Youth (Ages 10–17)		
	U.S.	Canada
murder	527	242
rape	13	2
robbery	199	95
aggravated assault	292	142

However, the difference between the U.S. and Canadian violent crime rates is diminishing; in the 1980s, the U.S. rate was nearly three times the Canadian rate.

The property crime arrest rates, for the United States and Canada are relatively similar. The U.S. arrest rate for larceny-theft was 70 percent greater than the Canadian rate—but the Canadian burglary arrest rate was 30 percent higher than the U.S. rate.

Arrests per 100,000 Youth (Ages 10–17)		
	U.S.	Canada
burglary	481	636
larceny	1,721	1,020
motor vehicle theft	311	238
arson	34	21

DEFINING THE TERMS

What's the difference between robbery, burglary, and larceny?

- Robbery is theft that takes place as the result of violence (or the threat of violence).
- Burglary means breaking and entering a building with the intent of committing a theft.
- Larceny is another word for theft; grand larceny involves the theft of an object worth more than a specified amount.

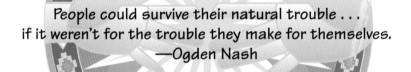

People could survive their natural trouble . . .
if it weren't for the trouble they make for themselves.
—Ogden Nash

2

CAUGHT

After the officers placed us in the backseat of the car, the older officer sat in the driver's seat. The other officer talked with the school janitors.

"This isn't good," Jeremy whispered to me. "It's the third time I've gotten caught."

I didn't know what to say, so I didn't say anything. My heart pounded, and I rubbed my sweaty hands on my jeans. I was scared, but I wasn't going to let Jeremy know.

Our little city is just that—little. It took only five minutes to drive to the police station. I had never been inside the station before. I had never had a reason to be there. We drove past the front of the building, around the side, and to the back parking lot. The older officer parked the car and walked to a door while the younger officer waited with us in the car.

"This is the juvenile door," he said. "We have sight and sound protection for you, which means all adult inmates cannot see or hear you.

A few minutes later the older officer came out and told us to follow him. Jeremy and I walked through the doorway into a hall—one officer in front of us, the other behind us. I could tell we were in the basement of the building because of the cement walls. I saw a red flashing light and a sign that read "JUVENILE IN ATTENDANCE."

"Are you going to put me in a cell?" Jeremy asked.

"No, juveniles cannot be put in cells at the police station," the older officer said.

"Are you going to cuff me to the wall?" Jeremy asked.

"No, that's only for adults," the officer answered.

The officer explained that sometimes an adult has to wait while sitting on a chair in the hallway. The defendant is handcuffed to a railing that is bolted into the hallway wall. But because Jeremy and I aren't adults, we will wait in a room with an officer.

I swallowed and could feel a lump in my throat. The officers walked us down the hall and into a designated area for juveniles. The younger office explained that in order for officers to ***interrogate*** juveniles, they must be in a room of a specific size, on the ground floor, and with a window. The older officer took Jeremy into one room, and the younger officer walked me into another room.

"Sit here." The officer pointed to a chair near the front door. He placed some papers on the desk in front of me. A few minutes later, another man walked into the room and sat behind the desk. I wasn't sure who he was because he wasn't in a uniform. He wore regular clothes and even a tie.

"Are you Ezekiel?" he asked.

"Zeek," I said.

"Okay, Zeek. I'm Detective Smith." He reached across the desk and stuck out his right hand to shake mine.

I raised my hands.

"You can take off his cuffs," Detective Smith said to the officer.

The officer removed my handcuffs and left the room. Then Detective Smith and I shook hands. I sat back in my chair.

"I need to contact your parents."

"They're at work."

"We can't discuss anything until you have a parent here with you. Where do they work?"

"My mom works at the hospital. My dad works at the shoe factory in shipping. He's hard to reach." I was hoping the detective would call my mom and not my dad.

"What's your mom's work number?"

I told the detective the number and waited as he dialed the phone.

"Mrs. Martinez? This is Detective Smith from the Riverside Police Department. This is not an emergency. We have your son Zeek—Ezekiel—here at the station."

I waited as he listened to my mother. Although I couldn't tell what she was saying, I could hear her high-pitched voice.

"He's fine. He wasn't in an accident. He was caught throwing rocks through a school window and is accused of criminal mischief. I need you or your husband to come down to the station."

Detective Smith talked with my mom a few more minutes, and then he hung up the phone.

"Is she crying?" I asked.

"Yes, she sounds upset. A lot of mothers are like that." Detective Smith pulled out a bunch of papers from a filing cabinet.

I looked around the room and noticed some pictures of officers and their families. The room looked neat and clean, and there was a strong odor of fresh paint. I thought the room looked good for being in a police station. The detective was busy writing, so I tried to act bored instead of showing I was nervous.

About thirty minutes later, I heard my parents talking to someone, their voices getting louder as they came closer to the room.

Oh great. Why'd she have to have Dad come?

They entered the room with an officer. I could tell my mom had been crying.

"Zeek, are you okay? Are you hurt?" She hugged me.

"Mom, I'm all right."

"Now what have you gone and done?" my father asked.

"Mr. and Mrs. Martinez, please sit down. I'm going to read the Miranda warnings, and I need you all to listen carefully," Detective Smith said.

My parents sat in chairs by the side of the desk. The officer closed the door and stood next to it.

"Ezekiel Martinez, you have the right to remain silent. You may refuse to answer questions. If you give up this right and talk with me, you may later change your mind and stop answering questions whenever you desire. Do you understand this right?"

"Yes," I said.

Detective Smith wrote my answer next to the question on the form. He read several more questions, slowly and deliberately, writing my answer next to each question.

"Please sign at the bottom of this form. I need one of your parents to sign, also."

After I signed the form, my father signed it. Detective Smith signed the form, and the officer signed as a witness. Then the officer left the room, closing the door behind him.

"Zeek, please tell me what happened—from the beginning," Detective Smith said.

I told the detective exactly what happened that evening. I never looked at my parents, especially when I talked about sneaking Dad's vodka. It didn't take long to tell the whole story.

"Now I need you to write down what you just told me." Detective Smith handed me a paper and a pen.

I don't know how long I spent writing my statement. Nobody talked while I wrote. When I finished, I looked at the detective.

"Zeek, have you ever been in trouble before?" Detective Smith asked.

"No," I said.

"And this better be the only time." I could hear the anger in Dad's voice.

"Mr. Martinez, let's try and stay calm," Detective Smith said.

My father crossed his arms, but thankfully he didn't say anything else.

"There are a few different ways we could go with this case," Detective Smith said. "Zeek, you may be a candidate for a **diversion program** through the youth court. That's a court of teen volunteers. Basically, youth court keeps you from proceeding through the juvenile court system, which we call family court. There are some requirements, though, in order to be accepted in youth court. It is available only to ***first-time offenders***. In addition, you have to plead guilty and complete your sentence. Also, your parents have to be willing to work with you to fulfill your obligations. If you agree to these conditions, I will contact the director of our youth court and give him the information."

"So it'll keep me from having a record?" I asked.

"Yes, if you're accepted into the program. If not, we can proceed with contacting the juvenile ***probation*** officer."

"I can do this youth court thing," I said.

"Mr. and Mrs. Martinez, do you agree to support this decision?" Detective Smith looked at my parents.

Dad looked at Mom. She nodded.

"Yes," Dad said.

"Then I'll contact the director. His name is Bob Larson. You can expect him to call you this weekend to set up an appointment. We're almost finished here, but there are a couple more things I want to show you. Follow me."

We walked out of the office and to a room at the end of the hallway. The red light was still blinking and the door to the other juvenile investigation room was closed. I assumed Jeremy was in there, but I didn't know for sure.

We entered a small room at the end of the hallway. One corner had a chair with a screen behind it. A few feet in front of it was a camera on a tripod.

"Is that where you take mug shots?" I asked.

"Yes," Detective Smith answered.

"Are you going to photograph my son?" Mom asked.

"No. Someone his age has to commit a ***felony***. Zeek has been charged with a ***misdemeanor***," Detective Smith said. "But I'm going to show Zeek what happens if he ever commits a felony."

Detective Smith showed me a card with a number. "This is for identification for our files. Because you are a juvenile, we will not use your name. You will only be identified by this number. It's another way to maintain your privacy. You'd hold this card at chest level and then we would take a picture."

It reminded me of TV shows. I imagined I would feel terrible—worse than being handcuffed.

"Come over here, please," he instructed.

We walked across a taped line on the floor.

"That's the line we have people walk on to see if they're under the influence of alcohol," Detective Smith said.

"Are you going to make him walk that line?" Mom asked.

"No," Detective Smith said.

He showed me a **breathalyzer** machine that the officers use to determine the alcohol content of an individual's breath sample.

We stayed in the room a few more minutes while Detective Smith explained the procedures for fingerprinting. I looked around the room and noticed a camera in a corner near the ceiling.

"This room is continuously monitored," Detective Smith said.

Besides being afraid, I felt humiliated. I was sure I'd feel worse if I had been fingerprinted and photographed. We walked down the hallway and to the juvenile door at the back of the building.

"Thank you for coming, Mr. and Mrs. Martinez." Detective Smith shook their hands.

"Thank you," Mom said.

"Remember, Mr. Larson will contact you this weekend."

"I'll make sure Zeek is home all weekend," Dad said.

"Zeek, stay out of trouble," Detective Smith said.

"Yes, sir," I said.

"Don't worry. This is the last time you'll see him." Dad gave me a look to make sure I understood what he meant.

We said good-bye and walked out of the police station.

DID YOU KNOW?

- In the United States, an officer of the law must read the Miranda rights to a juvenile.
- If the questioning of a juvenile is videotaped, an attorney must be present.
- An attorney must be present for the juvenile to participate in a police lineup.
- A juvenile usually is released to her parent or guardian. However, if there is need for protection or the charge is a felony, the minor may be put in a juvenile **detention** facility until the trial. Preventive detention is not inflicting punishment.

MIRANDA WARNINGS

Law enforcement officers should make sure that the juvenile understands his or her rights and the seriousness of the situation. Simply reciting the standard Miranda warnings is not good enough. Below is a sample of Miranda warnings for juveniles. Standard Miranda warnings are indicated by bold print.

1. **You have the right to remain silent.** You may refuse to answer questions. If you give up this right and talk with me, you may later change your mind and stop answering questions whenever you desire. Do you understand this right?
2. **Anything you say can and will be used against you in a court of law.** Anything you say may be used against you in family court. Do you understand this right?
3. **You have the right to have an attorney present before any questioning.** You have the right to talk with an attorney before speaking to me, and you may

have an attorney present during any questioning now or in the future. Do you understand this right?

4. **If you cannot afford an attorney, one will be appointed to represent you before any questioning.** If you want to have an attorney but cannot afford one, one will be provided for you without cost. Do you understand this right?

5. Do you understand these rights?

6. Now that I have advised you and your guardian or parent of your rights, are you willing to answer my questions without first talking with an attorney and having him present during questioning?

A police officer cannot arrest anyone without reading the individual the Miranda warnings.

If an adult who has been arrested becomes violent or unruly, his handcuffs may be fastened to a bolt like this one.

HISTORY OF MIRANDA WARNINGS

Ernesto Miranda was arrested in Arizona on charges of kidnapping and rape. After he had been identified in a police lineup, the police questioned Ernesto Miranda. Without first being told that he had the right to have a lawyer or that he had the right to remain silent, he confessed and signed a written statement. Miranda's confession was used at his trial and he was found guilty. The Arizona Supreme Court upheld the conviction.

In the case of *Escobedo v. Illinois* (1964), the U.S. Supreme Court had ruled that criminal suspects must be made aware of their right to consult a lawyer. However, that decision did not specify the exact procedures the police must follow to make sure a suspect's rights are not violated.

In 1966, the U.S. Supreme Court ruled on the landmark

Adult defendants may be handcuffed to a railing in the police station while they are waiting; juveniles, however, wait in a room with an officer.

case of *Miranda v. Arizona*. The ruling spelled out specific guidelines for police interrogation of criminal suspects held in custody. The Court ruled that the prosecution may not use statements made by a person under questioning in police custody unless certain minimum procedural safeguards were followed. The Court also said the prosecution could not use the statements obtained by the police while the suspect was in custody because the police had not made clear Miranda's right to not incriminate himself.

JUVENILE JUSTICE AND DELINQUENCY PREVENTION ACT OF 1974

This act provides the major source of federal funding to improve juvenile justice systems. It helps state and local gov-

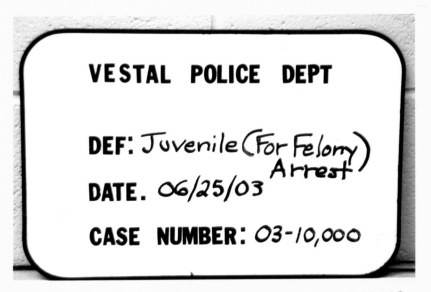

A sign like this one is used to identify the arrested individual for his "mug shot."

ernments, as well as individual and private organizations, to develop less costly, sensible, and more productive assistance for minors in the juvenile system. In order to receive federal funds, states are required to maintain these protections for children:

- Status offenders may not be held in secure detention or confinement.
- Juveniles may not be detained in adult jails and lockups except for limited times. (This does not apply to children who are tried or convicted in adult criminal court of a felony-level offense.)
- Sight and sound contact with adults is prohibited when juveniles are placed in an adult jail or lockup.
- States are required to gather information and assess the reason for *disproportionate* confinement of minority juveniles in all secure facilities.

HIRING A JUVENILE CRIME ATTORNEY

A juvenile may hire a lawyer at any stage of the case. She also has the legal right to represent herself, but this choice is not generally recommended. Before hiring a lawyer, the juvenile may want to learn:

- The lawyer's experience in this type of case.
- How much the entire case will cost.
- If there will be other juvenile defense lawyers working on the case.
- How the lawyer will inform the juvenile of the progress of the case.
- The lawyer's approach to the case.
- The possible outcomes of the case.
- The length of time it will take to resolve the case.

The police officer takes a picture of the defendant.

An office in the police station. A juvenile defendant might be interviewed here.

PUNISH THE PARENTS

Some U.S. states punish parents for the crimes committed by their children. This may be an attempt to make parents take some of the responsibility for their children's offenses. However, someone may question if this means good parents are taking the blame for something they did not do.

Here are a few cases to consider:

- Parents receive 160 hours of community service and a fifty-dollar fine if their children are caught possessing liquor, skipping school, or vandalizing.
- A mother served one hundred days in jail because her daughter missed fifty-nine days of school.
- A parent was cited for the son's shoplifting.

Are Parents Liable for Their Children's Acts?

Usually parents aren't financially responsible for their children's clumsy or **negligent** acts. Judges recognize that parents cannot prevent most childhood accidents and mishaps. However, parents may be liable if the injured person can show that the parents' failure to supervise the child directly caused the injury. Also, certain laws make parents liable for specific offenses.

WHO SENDS MINORS TO JUVENILE COURT?

Law enforcement **refers** most juvenile court cases. About half of the cases referred to juvenile court intake are handled informally.

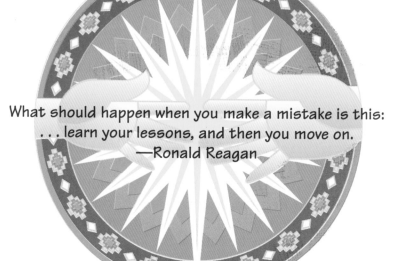

What should happen when you make a mistake is this:
. . . learn your lessons, and then you move on.
—Ronald Reagan

3

MISTAKES

As soon as we were in our car, my father started yelling. He turned around and jabbed his index finger directly at my chest as words spewed out of his mouth. I don't even remember what he said. I watched his finger poke the air, thankful he couldn't reach me. *God,* I thought, *please just let him shut up.* I don't remember everything he said, but I heard something about how I needed to put my hands to good use. Eventually, he ran out of words, turned around, started the car, and drove out of the parking lot. My stomach began to hurt like it was being tied in a knot. I wasn't sure if it was my nerves or just the alcohol wearing off.

Mom started crying again. She sounded like a whimpering puppy. "I'll call my manager and explain I won't be coming back to finish my double shift tonight. She won't be happy, but I don't think I will be able to concentrate. I'll ask if I can take the double shift next weekend."

I leaned my head against the back of my seat and closed my eyes until we pulled into our driveway. Then I went upstairs to my bedroom and opened my window, hoping the fresh air would help me relax. But since the houses in this neighborhood are so close to each other, I could hear my next-door neighbor snoring. I shut my window and listened to some music. Somehow, I finally fell asleep.

Late Saturday morning, Mom knocked on my bedroom door.

"You have a phone call." She handed me the phone.

"Hello?"

"Is this Ezekiel Martinez?" a man asked.

"Yeah, this is Zeek."

"Zeek, my name is Bob Larson, and I'm the director of the county youth court program. I understand you were picked up last night for criminal mischief."

"Yeah," I said.

"Is this is your first *offense*?"

"Yeah."

"I need to interview you and your parents before deciding whether to accept you in the program. Can you come to my office, or do I need to visit you at home?"

I put my hand over the phone and told my mom what Mr. Larson wanted. Eventually, we agreed to meet Monday at noon. Mr. Larson gave me directions to his office, and we said good-bye.

I took a shower and then went back to my bedroom. Even though I was upstairs, I overheard Mom downstairs, talking to my grandparents on the telephone. I wished she wouldn't tell everyone about the arrest. I didn't want anyone else to know. After Mom got off the telephone, I heard my little sister's voice.

"What happened to Zeek?" Jadira asked.

"He got arrested for chucking rocks through a school window," Dad's voice boomed, "and we had to leave work to go pick him up at the police station!"

"Jadira, please go play with Carlos," Mom said.

I heard both my younger brother and sister come upstairs. Carlos walked into my room, one step ahead of Jadira.

"Zeek, Dad said you got arrested!"

"Leave me alone," I said.

"You gonna go to jail?" Jadira asked.

"I don't know." *Maybe that'd be better than living here.*

"Oh, Zeek, I don't want you to get locked up." Jadira hugged my legs and started to cry. *She's just like Mom,* I thought. Their tears made my head ache.

Monday morning couldn't come fast enough. I didn't want anyone at school to find out why I was leaving early, so I didn't say anything to anyone. That wasn't hard, because no one talked to me, not even to say hi. My parents picked me up at school, and I ate lunch on the way to Mr. Larson's office.

Dad drove down Main Street and finally found a parking space on a side street. I put two quarters in the parking meter, hoping the meeting wouldn't be longer than two hours.

We walked across the street to the corner building. It was just like all the other old buildings in town—everything seemed old and run-down, like a gloomy, old hospital. We entered a waiting area lined with a bunch of cold plastic chairs. A few old magazines were scattered on the chairs and a corner table. There was no receptionist, so I peeked in an office and saw a man with papers all over his desk. His office didn't look any bigger than a closet.

He looked up at me. "Zeek?"

"Yes."

"I'll be with you in a minute."

After waiting only a couple minutes, Mr. Larson came out of his office and introduced himself. We followed him across the worn-out carpeting and into a conference room. Even though we were on the second floor, the air smelled musty, like our basement. The room reminded me of a little library with shelves of books and wooden chairs around a long rectangular wooden table. One wall caught my attention because it was lined with shelves of woodcarvings.

"I received some paperwork from Detective Smith of the Riverside Police Department. You were involved in an incident on Friday night at the school, throwing rocks at a window?" Mr. Larson asked.

"It was a little window in a door," I answered.

"Right. And you had been drinking vodka earlier that evening?"

"Yeah." I ducked my head and looked at the worn-out toes of my sneakers.

My father cleared his throat. I wasn't sure if he was angry with me, or if he was feeling uncomfortable because my mom now knew about his stash of booze in the shed.

"You were taken to the police station where you were read your Miranda rights, signed a consent form, and gave a written statement, correct?" Mr. Larson asked.

"Yeah."

"And you were released in your parents' custody?"

"Yeah."

"Let me explain about youth court. It is a diversion program, an alternative to the juvenile court system. The goal is to get involved early, when someone first shows **antisocial** behavior, and prevent more of this type of activity. It is a voluntary **peer** court system. Although there are hundreds of youth courts throughout the country, each has its own set of rules and **restrictions**. Our program is available only to first-time offenders between the ages of eleven and fifteen who have admitted their guilt. Youth court is strictly a **hearing** for sentencing purposes. You were charged with criminal mischief, right?"

"Yeah."

"We accept **property offenses**, but no violations to another person, such as assault."

"It was only property," I said. "Unless you consider the skeleton a person."

"No, we consider the skeleton an object." I thought maybe Mr. Larson was smiling just a little. "And since you didn't steal it, you weren't charged with that."

He continued to explain the program—youth court members are high school students who serve in the roles of judges, **prosecutors**, **defense counsels**, and court **bailiffs**. Mr. Larson and other staff members, as well as volunteer lawyers, are on hand to offer assistance and monitor court proceedings. After all the evidence is heard, the judges determine the sentence.

"It will be some type of community service, up to a hundred hours. There are a variety of places where you can serve. For example, we have programs for cleaning up parks, working at animal shelters, and helping at the library. I'll give you a list of organizations after the hearing. You can choose from the list or agree to the group activity on Saturday mornings."

"Okay." I stopped looking at my sneakers and sat up a little straighter.

"You will have no permanent record. Your case never goes to probation or family court. But you have to admit you're wrong. You may even have to write a letter of apology. There may be **restitution**. Also, you may have to attend some **behavioral** classes and visit some facilities."

"Like what?" I asked.

"One class is anger management. We visit a variety of places so you can learn what happens if you proceed in the juvenile court system. Many professionals, including judges, consider these visits very important."

"That sounds good to me," Dad said.

"Mr. and Mrs. Martinez, we have to have your cooperation in order to proceed. Are you willing to make sure Zeek has transportation to and from the places of community service?"

"Yes," Mom said.

"He's caused enough trouble. Maybe working on Saturdays will keep his nose clean." Dad glared at me.

"If Zeek fails to fulfill his sentence," Mr. Larson said, "he will be sent back to the traditional court system. This program teaches that there *are* consequences, and we seek to find ways to help the offender learn personal responsibility."

I nodded. "I think I can do this."

"Okay, let's fill out the paperwork. We hold court every Wednesday at the new courthouse. Do you know where that is?"

"It's behind the library," Mom said.

"Right. The address is on this form. Your hearing will be this Wednesday at six P.M. You need to arrive at five-thirty because you will be allowed thirty minutes to discuss your case with the defense counsel before the hearing begins. Do you have any questions?" Mr. Larson asked.

"Just one," I said.

"Go ahead, ask me anything."

"Did you make those?" I pointed to the woodcarvings.

"Yes, I made a couple of them. Kids in our program made some, too. Woodcarving is one of several classes we offer here at the community center. Would you like some information about it?"

I kept my eyes on those smooth pieces of wood and nodded.

Mr. Larson handed me a brochure and a pile of important-looking papers. "Zeek, many kids make mistakes. It doesn't mean it's the end of the world."

"No, I guess not," I said slowly, searching for the right words. "But it feels like being on the edge of disaster."

Mr. Larson looked at me, and I thought he understood what I was saying. All he said, though, was, "I'll see you Wednesday."

I didn't talk the entire ride home. Thankfully Dad didn't say anything either. But as usual, Mom cried.

THE JUVENILE MENTORING PROGRAM (JUMP)

JUMP is funded by the Office of Juvenile Justice and Delinquency Prevention (OJJDP). This program supports one-on-one mentoring projects for youth at risk. These risks include failing in school, dropping out of school, or involvement in juvenile delinquency, including gang activity and substance abuse. A **mentor** can be from public or private sectors.

Since 1994, more than 9,200 youth have received one-on-one mentoring. OJJDP has funded 203 JUMP sites in forty-seven states and two territories.

JUMP'S three principal goals are:

- Reduce juvenile delinquency and gang participation by at-risk youth.
- Improve academic performance of at-risk youth.
- Reduce the school dropout rate for at-risk youth.

A courtroom.

HELP FOR CHEYENNE YOUTH

The Bureau of Indian Affairs (BIA) is funding the building of Northern Cheyenne Youth Services Center in Busby, Montana. In addition to holding tribal court, this juvenile detention hall will also employ forty people. The tribe hopes to become involved early in the juvenile offenders' lives so they won't graduate to hard crime. In addition, the Youth Services Center will provide traditional Cheyenne healing and guidance for at-risk teens—something Indian teens don't get in non-Indian detention and counseling facilities.

The Boys & Girls Club also helps Northern Cheyenne children and teens improve their lives. Rather than going through the court system, teens who get in trouble can go through a juvenile diversion program. The program includes performing community service and attending mandatory drug and alcohol education programs. (From *Cheyenne* by Kenneth and Marsha McIntosh, Mason Crest Publishers, 2004.)

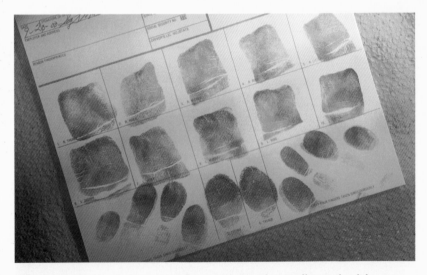

When a person is arrested for a crime, the police take his fingerprints.

Early concepts of justice demanded "an eye for an eye"; in other words, whatever a person did to someone else should be done to him. Today's juvenile justice system focuses more on preventing future crimes from being committed.

DIVERSION PROGRAMS

Many authorities state that the earlier a child enters the juvenile justice system, the greater the likelihood that he or she will develop and continue a delinquent and criminal career. For children who commit only minor offenses, several outstanding programs have helped communities use diversion.

- The Sacramento County Diversion Project offers a program titled Family Crisis Counseling: An Alternative to Juvenile Court. It is based on assisting the whole family as they deal with the problem. Trained probation officers meet with the family as soon as possible to provide crisis counseling, and a counselor helps to return the child home. As a result of the counselor's intervention, all family members make a commitment to work out the problem. These types of projects have four main goals:

1. To reduce the number of cases going to court.
2. To reduce the number of repeat offenses.
3. To decrease overnight detentions.
4. To achieve these goals at a cost equal to or less than that required for regular processing of cases.

- The Neighborhood Youth Resources Center in Philadelphia, Pennsylvania, provides a range of services for children who live in a high-crime area of the inner city.
- In New York City, Supported Employment for Adolescents (SEA) is another type of program that is an alternative to institutionalization. Court-referred juveniles between the ages of fourteen and sixteen work three hours a day in part-time jobs for which they are paid. In addition to the juveniles providing a valuable work service, they gain a spirit of dedication and of self-worth.

NATIONAL YOUTH NETWORK— VISION AND MISSION

The National Youth Network recognizes the importance of youth leadership. Through communication and action, youth and adults are united to provide opportunities for youth organizations and youth to have a positive impact in our communities.

The mission of the National Youth Network is to act as an agent that speeds significant change for youth across the country. The focus is on preventing crime and victimization and making a difference in their communities through:

- having youth-focused national, statewide, and community-based organizations work together
- distributing information
- advocating youth perspectives to policy makers
- using the media to promote youth activities
- reaching out to youth in the juvenile justice system

Youth can have a positive impact on their communities.

Everyone in the Youth Network is important. This unique partnership between kids and adults allows both parties to have rights and responsibilities.

- **Youth Committees** are the driving force behind the work of the Network. Actual work of the Network is accomplished through committees.
- **Sponsors** support teen members by providing

A person who has been arrested for a crime may feel shame and fear; organizations like the National Youth Network are designed to offer hope and fresh options to youth in trouble.

financial resources for the teen members to participate in national meetings. Sponsors also provide the technical and material resources to keep youth participating on a continuing basis. In addition, one or more designated adult staff within the organization is the contact person and the mentor to teen members.

- **The Leadership Council** is made up of three elected youth responsible for coordinating the activities of teen Network members, communicating with and between the Network committees, and communicating among teen members. The Council also exchanges thoughts, feelings, and information with the Office of Juvenile Justice and Delinquency Prevention (OJJDP) on behalf of the entire Network.

The final forming of a person's
character lies in his own hands.
—Anne Frank

4

YOUTH COURT

Time seemed to drag until late Wednesday afternoon. As soon as my mom got home from work, we ate dinner and then I helped with the dishes—without even being asked.

"Boy, you better learn something from this program, because I had to take a day's vacation from work to go to this court thing." My father took another swig of coffee.

It'd be nice for you to take a day off for me without it being a trial, I thought.

"You don't have to go. Mom can take me," I said.

"Your father and I are both going with you," Mom said. "We're a family. We'll get through this together. Now let's get ready. We need to leave early to drop off Carlos and Jadira. Your grandparents offered to watch them while we're at court."

I went upstairs and stood in front of my closet, looking at my clothes. *What does a kid wear to court?* I chose the same clothes I wore to church on Easter Sunday. I took one last look in the mirror. "Maybe looking like a church boy will help," I said to myself.

As we drove to the city courthouse, I think we stopped at every intersection. It was as if all the traffic lights were working against us. I

spotted the courthouse before we even turned into the parking lot—
it was the only new building in sight.

Nobody talked while Dad parked the car and we walked to the
courthouse. I wiped my sweaty hands on my jeans. I didn't know
why I was so nervous—this was just a bunch of kids like me. I
hoped no one knew me, though.

As soon as we entered the building, we were greeted by a police officer. "Empty your pockets and proceed through the metal detector."

Mom went first, and then I followed. Dad dropped his key ring
on the counter and walked under the metal arch. A red light flashed
and a loud buzzer sounded.

"Did you empty all your pockets, sir?" the officer asked.

Dad fished around in his jacket pocket and pulled out the court
papers that were fastened with a large paper clip. He set it on the
counter, walked back to the front door, and went through the detector again. This time there were no sirens or flashing lights.

"A stupid paper clip. This is ridiculous," Dad said.

He never lightens up, I thought.

Mr. Larson was waiting for us. "Hi, Zeek, Mr. and Mrs. Martinez."

"How long will this last?" Dad asked. "I don't want to spend my
whole night here."

I could feel my face get hot, but Mr. Larson didn't seem rattled.

"We're ready now. Zeek will meet with his defense counsel for
thirty minutes. Then we will proceed with the hearing, which can
be as short as fifteen minutes or as long as forty-five minutes. A lot
depends on how fast the kids speak. After the youth lawyers finish
presenting the case, the judges discuss the matter and decide on the
sentencing. They will announce the sentence, and I will answer any
of your questions. There are some papers you will need to sign. Each
case usually lasts about an hour, maybe a little longer. You should be
out of here by seven."

"Good," Dad said.

"Mr. and Mrs. Martinez, please have a seat in the back of the
room while I talk with Zeek."

My dad chose the chair closest to the door, and my mom sat next to him. Mr. Larson and I walked to the front of the room, and he introduced me to my **law guardian**. Jim was a little older than me. He was clean-cut, wearing new-looking clothes, including a tie, and shoes instead of sneakers, and he wrote some notes on lined yellow paper. *He even looks like a lawyer,* I thought.

We sat next to each other and reviewed my written statement, and Jim asked me a bunch of questions about what I did in my free time, if I had chores or helped around the house, if I baby-sat my brother and sister. We also talked about how often I drank alcohol and if I smoked pot or took other drugs. After we finished talking, I noticed the only adults in the room were my parents and Mr. Larson, who is at all the youth court hearings.

Three judges sat in the front of the room. I was surprised that not one of them wore a black robe. A high school student was the lawyer for the prosecution. She sat at one of the two tables. Jim and I sat at the other table. Another student served as the court bailiff. He stood next to the door—I guess to make sure no one entered the room.

One of the judges picked up the gavel and hit it on a little block of wood. "Court is in session," she said.

"Case Number 729-03, State versus Ezekiel Martinez," the court bailiff said.

The attorneys each gave an opening statement.

"Your Honors," the prosecutor began, "I would like to present Exhibit 1, which is the officer's written statement regarding this incident."

"No objection," Jim said.

"Accepted," another judge said.

The court bailiff placed a label on the back of the report. The prosecutor presented some more **evidence**, but everything related only to sentencing since I had already admitted my guilt.

"Prosecution rests," the girl lawyer finally said.

"I call Ezekiel Martinez to the stand," Jim said.

I sat in the witness chair next to the judges. The court bailiff told me to raise my right hand to take an oath, promising that what I would say is true. I did.

Jim proceeded to ask me the same questions he had asked during our private discussion. When he finished, the prosecutor asked only a few questions—to clarify a couple points—about how often I drank and if I skipped school. I told her I drank only on Friday nights, but not every week, and that I never skipped school. I didn't get straight A's, but I tried my best. I didn't mention that I was scared what my dad would do if I ever bombed a test or cut a class.

After I finished testifying, each lawyer gave a closing argument. The prosecutor talked about my drinking; she mentioned that I didn't have any social activities, other than hanging out with Jeremy, and she recommended a sentence of sixty to seventy hours of community service. She also recommended drug and alcohol rehab classes.

Jim talked about how responsible I was, that I was not *truant*, or absent from school without permission, that I got good grades, that I helped around the house with chores, and that sometimes I baby-sat Carlos and Jadira. He acknowledged that I willingly participated in the offense of throwing rocks and breaking the window, but he pointed out that I did not enter the school building, and I had nothing to do with stealing the skeleton. He recommended a lesser sentence, thirty to forty hours of community service.

The judges left the room. A few minutes later they came back and announced my sentence.

"Ezekiel Martinez," one judge announced, "we hereby sentence you to twenty to twenty-four hours of community service, ten to twelve hours behavioral classes including alcohol rehabilitation, and fifteen to twenty hours of visiting justice system personnel and facilities. The combined time of sentence is fifty hours. This allows some flexibility in scheduling the various activities."

"Thank you, Your Honors," Jim said.

"Thank you, Judges," the prosecutor said.

"Thank you," I said.

"Court is ***adjourned***," one judge said. He struck the little wooden block with the gavel.

Mr. Larson asked my parents and me to sign some forms, agreeing that I had participated in this youth court and that I agreed with the sentence. Then he gave me a copy of the papers, along with a list of community service programs.

"I recommend you begin this Saturday morning in a group activity. We're cleaning up the school grounds. Wear clothes you don't mind getting dirty, and be at my office at eight A.M. Saturday morning." He smiled. "And if you're interested, you can start a woodcarving class that afternoon."

"I'll think about it," I said.

"You can let me know Saturday morning. Just bring a lunch if you plan to stay for the class."

We said good-bye, and Mr. Larson began talking with the youth court participants. My parents and I walked to our car. Before my dad had even started the engine, he turned around and jabbed his index finger in the air.

"You'd better not screw up again," he said.

I wanted to grab that finger and break it, but I didn't say or do anything.

YOUTH COURT

Sometimes called peer courts, teen courts, or school courts, this diversion program offers an alternative to the juvenile justice system. Police, probation, schools, or family court can refer offenders. Local government agencies, juvenile probation offices, nonprofit organizations, youth and recreation services, and schools may organize and operate youth courts. Typical cases include shoplifting, drug and substance abuse, and criminal mischief.

Because the **respondent** admits guilt, the police officer advises her of the option to go to youth court instead of juvenile court. If the respondent chooses to go to juvenile court, she may be placed on probation. If the respondent goes before the youth court, other teenagers will judge her. In addition to admitting guilt, the respondent must be willing to carry out the sentence determined by her peers.

The sentence:

- Educates the respondent about the impact of her actions on other people and the community.
- Holds the respondent accountable for her actions.
- May include community service, restitution, counseling and educational classes, and letters of apology.

Some youth court sentences include participating in future youth court cases. In other youth courts, many offenders complete their sentence and then volunteer to serve on future youth court cases. By allowing offenders to participate in youth court, they learn they are valuable and can help others. It also encourages the youth to stop looking at themselves as offenders and to consider themselves valuable contributors in their community.

Who Participates in Youth Court?

- First-time nonviolent offenders.
- Teen volunteers who serve as judge, jurors, prosecutor, defense attorney, bailiff, or clerk—some courts have more than one judge, some courts do not have jurors, and some courts have real lawyers who volunteer their services.
- An adult serves as the teen court coordinator.

A person who appears in court swears to tell the truth.

Are All Youth Courts the Same?

No. All youth courts follow the same purpose—youth sentencing their peers. However, there are differences such as: the structure of the hearings, the type of cases they handle, the age of respondents and volunteers, how often they hold hearings each month, the number of cases per year, the amount and type of training volunteers receive, and the sentencing guidelines they follow.

The judge listens to evidence and tries to make a fair decision; youth court judges do the same for their peers.

The judge's sentence is based on the evidence and sentencing guidelines.

As of March 2003, there are approximately nine hundred youth court programs operating in forty-six states and the District of Columbia.

New York operates more than eighty-five youth courts throughout the state, representing more than 10 percent of the youth courts in the United States.

DON'T SKIP SCHOOL!

According to William Ayers, author of *A Kind and Just Parent*, kids who are chronically truant—in other words, kids who make a habit of skipping school—are more apt to end up in juvenile court.

WORDS YOU MAY HEAR IN COURT

accessory: Someone who helps another person commit or try to commit a crime before the fact, but who is not present when the crime takes place.

accomplice: Someone who joins with another to commit a crime; the accomplice bears equal responsibility under the law.

adjudication: The sentence or decision handed down by the judge.

appeal: A request to a superior court to reverse the decision of a lower court or to grant a new trial.

arraignment: A court procedure where formal charges are brought against a defendant, who is advised of his or her constitutional rights and may have the opportunity to offer a plea.

assault: A threatened or attempted physical attack in which the attacker appears to have the ability to bring about bodily harm if not stopped. **Aggravated assault** involves an attack that is done with recklessness and the intent to injure someone seriously, or an assault with a deadly weapon. **Battery** is assault in which the attacker makes actual contact.

breaking and entering: Illegal entrance with the intent to commit a crime. Simply pushing a door open and walking in can be breaking and entering.

brief: A document in which a lawyer makes his or her client's case by raising legal points and citing authorities.

corroborating evidence: Additional evidence that backs up proof already offered.

damages: A court-ordered monetary award to someone who was hurt by another.

disorderly conduct: A wide range of offenses, such as drunkenness or fighting, that disturb the public peace.

After hearing all the evidence, the judge will decide whether the adult defendant is guilty or not guilty. Juvenile respondents, however, are usually "admitted" into the system, rather than being considered "guilty."

docket: A list of cases to be tried by a court; its calendar.

felony: A serious crime, usually punishable by a prison term. A **misdemeanor** is a less serious crime.

in camera: A judicial meeting which the public cannot attend.

negligence: Acting carelessly, without reasonable caution, and thereby putting another person at risk.

perjury: The act of lying under oath.

protective custody: The imprisonment of an individual for his or her own protection.

public defender: A lawyer provided by the state to an accused person who cannot afford or who refuses counsel.

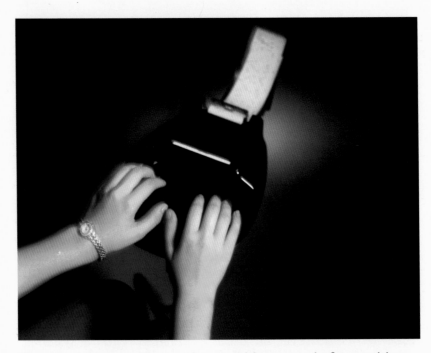

The court stenographer makes a written record of everything that is said during legal proceedings.

release on one's own recognizance: When an accused person promises to appear in court and is let go without having to provide bail.

self-incrimination: Under the Fifth Amendment of the Constitution, a person cannot be forced to make a statement that implies his or her own guilt.

statutory rape: A criminal offense that involves sex with a girl who is under the age of legal consent (the age varies in different legal jurisdictions).

summons: Notice to appear in court as a defendant in a law suit.

youthful offender: A person who can no longer be legally considered a juvenile, but whom the judge decides should not yet be treated as an adult.

God, grant me the serenity to accept the things I cannot change, courage to change the things I can, and the wisdom to know the difference.
—Reinhold Niebuhr

5

STEPS TOWARD SERENITY

The following Saturday morning, Dad and I arrived at Mr. Larson's office at a quarter to eight in the morning.

"I'm guessing you're planning to stay for the woodcarving class." Mr. Larson pointed to my lunch.

"I thought I'd see what it's about," I said.

"Mr. Martinez, you can pick up Zeek here at five this afternoon."

My dad left without saying anything. I sat on one of the cheap plastic chairs in the waiting area. Soon three other kids arrived—two girls and one guy—and Mr. Larson drove us to the school. We spent all morning picking up trash and washing off chalk markings from the sidewalk. At first I didn't talk with anyone. But while we were working, a kid named Derek asked me about my sentence. He told me this was his first day of community service, too. He had been sentenced to sixty hours because he was caught with a small amount of marijuana.

◈

Several of us were finished eating when Mr. Larson walked into the dingy community center waiting room. He talked about the different classes the center offered on Saturday afternoons. I wondered if anyone was forced to take one of these classes as part of his youth court sentence. Derek was taking the woodcarving class, too. I was glad I wasn't the only one.

Mr. Larson drove us to a home on the outskirts of the county. As soon as we stepped onto the front porch, an old wrinkled man got up from a rocking chair and shook our hands.

"Derek and Zeek," Mr. Larson said, "I'd like to introduce you to Mr. Barton. He owns this property, and he's your woodcarving instructor."

Leaning on a walking stick, Mr. Barton led us to a side hill with a bunch of small trees. He told us he has all his woodcarving students each select a sapling from this hill. He explained that when a tree is on a side hill, the root grows and forms a right angle so the tree can grow toward the sun. For our woodcarving project, we needed a young hardwood tree, about an inch or inch and a half in diameter, with the root attached.

Mr. Barton handed each of us a small gardening shovel and a sharp hatchet. He told us to choose a sapling, dig to find the root, and then cut the root about six inches from the right angle. Although both our saplings were sort of gnarled, each was about four feet long, with a definite right angle and a six-inch extension of root.

We walked back to the shed, and Mr. Barton explained that when the saplings are green, the bark strips off easily. He showed us how to take a carving knife and with long downward strokes, remove the bark. After that, he told us to place our roots onto a pile of other roots.

"These need time to dry before anyone can carve them. It'll take at least a year."

"A year! So how are we gonna carve something?" Derek asked.

"Those were cut last year by other students." Mr. Barton pointed to a pile of saplings. "Next year at this time, someone will be able to use the ones you cut today. It's a cycle—make a choice, learn from the experience, and help someone else."

He explained about the different types of wood to use for carving. Although we needed hardwood for our main project, when we learned the basic woodcarving strokes we would use softwood, since it is easy to cut. He gave us each a block of basswood and had us draw the figure of a fish on it, the top and side viewpoints. Then he taught us the five basic carving techniques.

Even though my cutting strokes weren't even, I could tell it was a fish, so I felt pretty good. Mr. Barton finished the lesson by telling us this week we were to sketch some ideas of how we wanted to carve the six-inch section of root. We thanked him and left.

On the ride back to town, I wondered who was picking me up. If my dad ever asked me about anything, his questions were usually followed by yelling or finger-jabbing. The best I could wish for was that he didn't say anything. But my mom—well, I knew she'd ask about my day and probe me until I gave her some details. Even though I never let her know, I like when she needles me for more information. I hoped she was waiting for me.

Mr. Larson parked his car. "I'll see you both on Tuesday afternoon for our first field trip. After that, we'll return to the community center for a drug and alcohol rehab class."

As I crossed the street toward our car, I noticed my father in the driver's seat.

I muttered a swear word—and then I took a deep breath, bracing myself for the next finger-jabbing and yelling session.

After school on Tuesday my mom dropped me off at the community center. Mr. Larson was waiting for me, along with Derek and the two girls. As part of our sentences, we were going to meet a juvenile probation officer.

We went downtown and parked on the third level of one of the parking ramps. Then we walked across a catwalk to the County Office Building. We rode an elevator up to the fourth floor and entered the Probation Department offices.

Soon a young woman named Ms. McCormick invited us to sit

at a round table. Her office reminded me of Mr. Larson's—piles of brown legal folders on her desk and even stacked on the floor. Ms. McCormick introduced herself and said she was a probation officer. She said because we were in a diversion program, we would be meeting only with her today. She emphasized that she expected this would be the only time she'd ever meet any of us.

Ms. McCormick explained the purpose of probation and what is expected of a respondent. She told us a respondent is usually contacted every week. She talks with the kid about behavior and other stuff—like we have to tell our probation officer about our activities, she makes sure we're meeting **curfew**, and we have to ask her before we can travel out of town. It actually sounded the same as my parents' rules. But for kids who didn't have those sorts of rules in their home, I guess probation may seem hard.

After that meeting, we returned to the community center. The drug and alcohol rehab meeting was on the first floor. I walked into another dingy room that smelled damp. I saw Derek already sitting on one of the chairs that were arranged in a circle, so I sat next to him. The leader explained the format and pointed out a few other things, like where the bathrooms and the exits were located.

The atmosphere felt as cold as the seat of my metal folding chair. It got a little more comfortable throughout the meeting, though. At first we went around the room and said our names, our ages, and why we were there. Some of us were there for drinking alcohol. A couple kids were there because they got caught smoking pot.

The leader gave us some paper and pencils to take notes, and then she rattled on about **twelve steps**. The meeting lasted an hour. Every once in a while someone would answer a question or share a story, but I never said anything besides the information at the beginning.

I took a few notes, but I didn't pay close attention to what she was saying. I was busy looking at the posters hung around the room. One poster especially caught my attention. When the meeting ended and everyone was leaving, I quickly copied the words from the poster onto the back of my notes. I wrote:

"The Serenity Prayer—God, grant me the serenity to accept the things I cannot change, courage to change the things I can, and the wisdom to know the difference."

I was glad to see my mom waiting for me in our car. As long as she wasn't crying, I expected a pleasant evening before my dad got home from work.

The next Saturday morning we went back to the school and began working at the school playground. I didn't know all the other kids yet, so Derek and I worked together. I was glad, because I sure didn't want to work with this one particular girl. She pretended to be busy, but she didn't do much of anything. When she actually did work, she complained. This week she whined because she broke a fingernail! I tuned her out and helped Derek install a tire swing. We worked hard to get the three chains even so the tire would be balanced. After we finished, I stood back and looked at what we'd done, and then I smiled and gave Derek a high-five. I don't actually remember the last time I had such a good day. We went back to the community center and ate our lunches.

That afternoon Derek and I continued with our woodcarving lessons. We sat on the porch and carved while Mr. Larson and Mr. Barton talked. I used the techniques he had taught us the previous week. We worked for four hours, and by that time I had a nasty blister.

THE SURVEY THAT STARTED IT ALL

Across the United States, youth have been telling the Department of Justice that they are concerned about crime and violence in their schools and communities. The 1995 report, *Between Hope and Fear: Teens Speak Out on Crime and the Community,* describes youths' views on how crime and violence affect their lives and whether youth are willing to participate in activities designed to oppose crime and violence.

More than two thousand students in grades seven through twelve participated in the survey about violence and crime. Students from both private and public schools responded as follows:

- 29 percent are worried about being victimized.
- 46 percent have made at least one change in daily routines because they are concerned about personal safety, crime, and violence in their communities.
- 40 percent report being in a physical fight with another youth in the past year.
- 29 percent said it is "very easy" to get illegal drugs in their neighborhoods; another 31 percent said that getting drugs was "somewhat easy or not very hard."
- 21 percent said that belonging to a gang was "like having a family" that would "always be there."
- 86 percent of those surveyed said that they were willing to participate in crime prevention/crime reduction programs within their communities.

Many teens find that crime and violence have a negative effect, yet these teens believe that they can make a positive difference.

Early-intervention programs are designed to keep kids from getting in trouble.

AN OUNCE OF PREVENTION

Early intervention tends to help children who may be at risk of violence either as perpetrators or victims. Community-based youth service organizations provide various prevention, intervention, and diversion programs for youth. The following are some examples:

- accessible drug- and alcohol-treatment programs
- alternatives to institutions for juvenile offenders
- mentoring and esteem-building programs
- peer counseling, support, and recreation
- safe youth shelters and drop-in centers
- skill building in education and employment

WHAT TYPES OF CASES ARE HEARD IN FAMILY COURT?

- child neglect and abuse
- child support
- adoption
- custody
- domestic violence
- guardianship
- juvenile delinquency
- paternity
- termination of parental rights
- visitation

Computer technology allows the important members of legal proceedings to see visual evidence.

There are many kinds of courtrooms.

There is no typical juvenile court scene. If the juvenile is found delinquent, the hearings consist of two parts:

- The *fact-finding phase* is the part of a juvenile hearing that determines whether or not a juvenile is delinquent.
- A *dispositional hearing* is a hearing in which a judge concentrates on the best interests of the child while protecting the community.

PROBATION VERSUS SUPERVISION

Theoretically, there is a difference between probation and supervision. But the difference tends to be more abstract than real, and in practice, the two amount to the same thing.

Some city court buildings are big and fancy, while the court buildings in smaller communities may be smaller and less imposing—but the legal proceedings will be very similar in either case.

Probation is a period of supervision after *admitting* or confessing that something is true.

Supervision is a period of supervision after *denial* or saying something is not true.

As the kindly parent, the state is supposed to act in the best interest of the child. In many cases, a child breaks laws that apply only to young people. Children who break such laws are called status offenders. In some states these children are considered to need supervision. They are labeled as PINS (person in need of supervision). Some states refer to these children as MINS (minor in need of supervision) or CHINS (child in need of supervision).

Juveniles who are placed on probation will usually be required to attend school and complete their academic requirements.

Juveniles often have their own rooms where they are interviewed in court buildings and police stations.

Juveniles placed on probation also receive other dispositions. The probation order may include additional requirements such as:

- Drug counseling
- Weekend confinement in the local detention center
- Community or victim restitution

The Juvenile Probation Violation Court is the nation's first court focusing on delinquent youth assigned to intensive probation. The court handles cases exclusively from the New York City Department of Probation's intensive supervision program for juvenile delinquents. The court serves as the center of communication between several agencies involved in juvenile probation cases. Probationers are required to appear regularly before a judge, who can impose sanctions—such as increased reporting, electronic monitoring, curfews, and home confinement—to encourage probationers to behave responsibly. As well, the judge can offer incentives—rewards such as recreational, educational, and training opportunities.

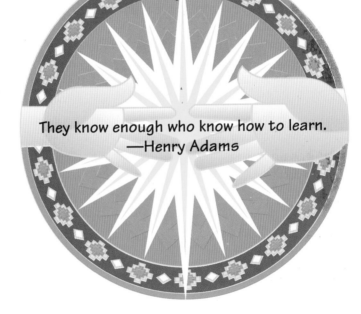

They know enough who know how to learn.
—Henry Adams

6

LEARNING MORE

I attended another drug and alcohol rehab class on Tuesday. This week we discussed why people sneak alcohol. I learned Jeremy and I weren't the only ones who played "hide-n-drink." I actually spoke during the class—I said that the reason I drank vodka was because it doesn't have an odor, so my parents couldn't smell it on my breath. I figure that's why my dad has vodka instead of a different kind of alcohol. Some kid said it was the first time he heard this. I was surprised, because I thought everyone knew that already.

At the end of the class, a few of the kids were talking about a girl who had been at last week's class, but she wasn't here today. Someone said she had run away over the weekend, and no one had seen or heard from her yet. I wondered if anyone even searched for her.

This week, our field trips were to two residential facilities. We have several in our county, but the first one we visited was Palmer Non-Secure Detention Facility. Most kids who arrive there go through detention for the first week. The detention building is separate from the rest of the campus, and only twelve kids stay there. The adults try to make the field trip a realistic experience, so the first thing they did was handcuff us before we got out of the car because sometimes kids arrive handcuffed. I'd never let anyone know, but being handcuffed really bothers me. I feel so ashamed and scared, but I either don't say anything at all or I act like it's no big thing.

Even though it's a non-secured detention facility, the front door is always locked. We waited on the porch while the director unlocked the door. Once inside, the police officer took off our handcuffs and escorted us into a small office where there's always a staff member on duty. Usually, more than one staff member is there, but sometimes the director is the only one.

She took our jackets and shoes, explaining that's how they **deter** residents from escaping. I'm sure it works in the winter with all the snow we have here. After they locked up our shoes and coats, the director explained a bunch of rules. There's a point system with four levels—white, yellow, red, and blue being the highest. At orientation, every resident starts out at the white level. After a resident reaches one level, he can earn enough points to go to the next level. The director said this program is fun if residents can respect people and follow simple directions. Then the residents will get privileges. "Life is about privileges," she said.

Palmer House, as the director called it, is an old brick house that doesn't look like an institution. There's a living room with a bookshelf full of board games and puzzles. The dining room has two big tables, like my grandmother's wooden table. The kitchen looked like a regular kitchen except here the food is always locked up. In the director's office is the "Closet Store." It's really a closet that has shelves filled with little items. Once a resident reaches the red level, he can use his points to buy some of the items. I'm not sure what I'd buy, because the first thing I saw was a shelf with various types of makeup.

Walking down the hall, I noticed the "Caught Ya!" board. The director explained that it's to encourage good behavior, like using polite manners or being kind to someone. The trick is that a resident has to do it without pointing it out to anyone beforehand. Once a resident is caught in the act of kindness or goodness, then the staff member writes out a ticket and puts it on the board. Each ticket is worth a certain amount of points, which helps in raising the resident's progress to a higher color.

When a resident reaches the blue level, she can have the privilege of going to the basement. That's where there's a TV, computers, and exercise equipment. Kids are not allowed access to the Internet, but they can at least play computer games. They also are allowed e-mail through the school.

The bedrooms and bathrooms are upstairs. The bedrooms are bare except for a single bed and small dresser. All the doors are unlocked. And if a resident is in her room, the door has to remain open. A staff member always sits in the hallway—even when kids are sleeping.

The director seemed tough. I wouldn't want to argue with her. But she was also nice. She said she tells all the residents that they're not bad kids because they're here, and that the staff likes the residents, but now the residents need to improve their behavior.

No one really stays in this detention home for long. Respondents usually have a court hearing within a few days and learn where they'll be going from there. Sometimes they stay at Palmer House, but in the residential program where they will attend classes and live in the dorms. Some kids go to other places, like a secured facility. I guess there are even kids who return home after a while.

The second juvenile home we visited that week is a maximum secured facility for boys, ages fourteen to twenty-one. We drove to a back road in a wooded section about forty-five minutes from our little city. A high fence with triple wire on the top surrounded the **compound**. The few buildings looked like one-story brick office buildings. This place definitely looked like a prison. All the windows had bars on the outside, and I saw security guards everywhere. First we had to stop at the gate and get permission to enter. At the main building, we had to go through a metal detector. That's when I first saw a group of guys walking down the hall. They all wore the same type of clothing, like a uniform—navy blue shirts, khaki

pants, and white running shoes. The only difference was the different colors of their shoelaces. I learned each shoelace color represents
the level of progress for that boy.

Although the guys were talking with each other, only a few
smiled. As they got closer, I noticed many of them had scars on their
hands, arms, and faces. I wondered if they're like most teenagers in a
group, wanting to act like everybody else.

Besides having so many guards, the center also has strict rules. I
was surprised there were so many classes. The administrator who
gave us the tour said they try to help the boys develop their skills
and knowledge so they can succeed when they get out. Some profes-
sors from a nearby college and other adults volunteer to come and
teach the boys. We walked past a few classrooms where boys were
learning computer skills, math, science, and reading. It reminded
me of school—except for the guard in each class.

The administrator also said this is more than a prison; it's a
school, a home, and may even be one of the safest places some of
these boys have ever lived. He said this center is considered a model
facility, and some kids say they feel safer here than at other secure facilities. But I thought even with my dad always losing his temper,
my home is definitely safer than there.

We continued community service on Saturday. This week we
painted the wooden playground structure. I was in charge of "the
castle" as my little sister calls it. I painted it bright yellow.

This week's woodcarving lesson was almost a repeat of the previous Saturday. Now I could see that the curved portion began to look
like my design. I was carving it into the shape of a black bass. Derek
was carving an eagle.

I was relieved when I saw my mom waiting to pick me up instead of my dad. But as soon as I got in the car, I knew something
was wrong. She was crying.

"Your father hurt his leg," she told me as soon as I got in the car. "The doctor has him on crutches for a while. They're watching for a blood clot."

"How did it happen?"

"He slipped while he was mowing the lawn."

"Oh." I looked out the window. I didn't want her to know that my dad had told me to mow the lawn earlier that week. He said it would be a way to do something good with my hands. Now I expected he would say it was my fault that he got hurt.

RESIDENTIAL PLACEMENT

The judge may order a juvenile to be committed to a residential placement for a specific period of time. In many states, the judge commits a juvenile to the state department of juvenile corrections, and it's the department's responsibility to determine where the juvenile will be placed and when he will be released.

Secure facilities provide intensive programming for youth requiring a highly controlled and restrictive environment. In New York, these facilities are located in non-urban areas, and all program services are provided on the grounds.

Limited secure facilities are used for youth previously placed in secure facilities as a first step in their transition back to the community. Most of these facilities in New York are located in rural areas, and all program services are provided on the grounds.

Non-secure facilities are both urban and rural residential centers and community-based programs. New York facilities range in size from a ten-bed community residential home to a sixty-bed rural residential facility.

Day placement programs are offered as alternatives to traditional residential placement in New York. In these programs, youth live in their homes and receive intensive supervision and services.

Arthur J. Audy Home

Audy Home is a detention center for children who must be incarcerated because it is "in their best interests." It provides temporary shelter for children awaiting trial on delinquency charges. Most children there either have committed very serious criminal offenses, such as murder or armed robbery, or are neglected or have run away. So the Audy Home houses children who have done very bad things and those whose parents have abandoned them.

New York House of Refuge

Established in 1824, the New York House of Refuge was the first center for the forcible detention of wayward children in the United States. The motivation was based on the idea that troubled children should be removed from the fate that awaited them in adult prisons.

Unless they are tried as adults, juvenile offenders do not go to prison; they may be placed in a residential facility instead.

This institution came through the efforts of two men. James W. Gerard was a young lawyer who had defended a fourteen-year-old boy accused of stealing a bird. Gerard won. The boy was *acquitted* because Gerard argued that prison would corrupt him. Gerard was so interested in this case he began investigating New York prison facilities for juveniles. He joined a society that was interested in reforming juvenile delinquents.

Isaac Collins was a Quaker who was a member of the Society for the Prevention of Pauperism. In 1822, with Gerard's help, Collins prepared a report that led to the creation of the New York House of Refuge.

This minimum-security detention facility looks like any other house in the neighborhood.

Way Stations

Detention centers are intended to operate as a stopping place between the time a child is accused and the time of a hearing when secure custody is needed. However, sometimes detention is lengthy and the experience is traumatic and weakens the child's morale.

RUNAWAYS

The National Runaway Switchboard (NRS) offers assistance to youth—those who are considering running away or have run away—and their families. The NRS helps join youth and their families to programs and resources, to crisis counseling, and to each other, as appropriate.

The NRS offers the following services:

- A confidential, toll-free hot line. Hot line staff and volunteers provide crisis intervention counseling.
- Referrals from callers to community-based programs and services across the country.
- Message delivery service between youth and their families or guardians.
- Conference calls facilitated by hot line staff and volunteers among parents, youth, and resource agency staff.
- An Internet Web site—http://www.nrscrisisline.org. In addition to promoting NRS services and highlighting its partnerships, the site also offers links to other Web sites as well as national and state demographic information on youth who have contacted NRS.

The intake office in a minimum-security detention facility for juveniles.

Home Free

In 1995, the National Runaway Switchboard (NRS) became the sole administrator of the HOME FREE Program in which Greyhound Lines, Inc. and the International Association of Chiefs of Police work together. Through HOME FREE, runaways who desire to return to their families are provided with free transportation to their homes.

Some Important Numbers

- National Runaway Hot Line: 1-800-621-4000 TDD (for callers who are deaf): 800-621-0394
- National Runaway Hot Line: 1-800-231-6946
- Texas National Runaway Hot Line (formerly known as Operation: Peace of Mind): 1-800-392-3352
- Boys Town National Hot Line: 1-800-448-3000; TDD: 1-800-448-1833
- Covenant House Nineline: 1-800-999-9999
- National Youth Crisis Hot Line: 1-800-442-HOPE (442-4673)
- Just For Kids Hot Line: 1-888-594-KIDS
- National Youth Crises Hot Line: 1-800-782-7335
- Suicide Prevention Hot Line: 1-800-827-7571

Better a mistake at the beginning than at the end.
—African saying

7

LIVING WITH
THE CONSEQUENCES

The next few days were brutal. My dad barked orders all the time. I was glad I had to go to Mr. Larson's class this week.

When I arrived at the community center, Mr. Larson told me today's class was not drug and alcohol rehabilitation. The subject was anger management.

"My dad should be here," I muttered.

I followed Mr. Larson into a room I had not been in before. I guess someone tried to make us feel comfortable because there were no cold metal chairs. There weren't even plastic chairs. There were four sofas. The cushions must have been threadbare because sheets were draped over the sofas. They were probably meant to look like slipcovers, but the room looked more like what I see in scary movies—a creepy old house with cobwebs and sheets covering the furniture. I plunked down on one end of a sofa and waited.

Mr. Larson led this session. It wasn't too bad. He talked about the reasons we get angry and some ways people express their anger. He even explained the difference between mad and angry. I had never thought about it before—that the word "mad" means insane while "angry" means showing anger. He also talked about reactions. I wished my dad heard the lesson. When the class ended, we went with Mr. Larson on a field trip.

"This week we're going to the county jail," he said.

It can't be any worse than that secured facility, I thought.

95

"I'd like you to pay attention to any differences between the jail and the juvenile facilities," Mr. Larson said.

Our old county jail had run out of space, so we now had a newly built one a few miles from the downtown area. The jail had wires around a big blacktopped area, which looked like a playground without slides or swings. There were a couple basketball hoops but no nets.

The part of the facility we walked through reminded me of the secured juvenile center we visited last week. The only difference I saw was that here all the inmates were adults wearing orange jump-suits.

It was a brief tour. I shuddered every time I heard the bars clang shut. I wondered how anyone ever gets used to that noise. We drove back to the community center in silence. I said nothing—not even to my mother who was waiting to pick me up.

Thursday I was excused a couple hours early from school so I could go on the next field trip. We were to spend the afternoon in one of the courtrooms, not a family court or juvenile court or town court. This was criminal court, where the trials were for felonies; where the defendant, if convicted, could go to prison for a long time—maybe even for life.

Mr. Larson and two other staff members drove twelve of us downtown. It was the same set of buildings where we had met with the probation officer. We walked up the old cement stairs, past the columns on the front porch, and entered through enormous wooden doors. Before we could even walk down the hall, one by one we walked through a metal detector. *There's probably one of these in every courthouse now,* I thought.

We went to a large waiting room, almost like a holding area. I estimated at least a hundred people were there. I recognized a girl from school who was slumped over with her legs wrapped around the aluminum chair legs. She looked so pathetic, like a rag doll that no one wanted. I turned away before she looked up. I didn't want her seeing me there. And I didn't want her knowing I saw her.

Mr. Larson pointed us toward a row of chairs. I was the last one seated, and soon a little girl sat next to me.

"Hi." She was smiling so much her face looked shiny. "My name is Beth. This is my mommy and daddy. They're adopting me today. The judge is gonna make us a real family."

I smiled back at her. It felt good seeing someone happy sitting in a courthouse. Everyone else looked angry, bored, or sad. Some people were even crying. After waiting about fifteen minutes I heard a voice on a loudspeaker. "Mr. Larson and students, please go to Courtroom 15."

We all walked out of that room and down the hallway. I was surprised to see modern furniture, because the outside of this courthouse looked ancient. It has a big dome top and a huge clock that you can see all over downtown.

Although the courtroom furniture was modern, everything else was what I expected. The judge's bench was on a little platform at the front. Next to him was the witness box. A court reporter was sitting at a stenograph. She pressed the keys on that little black machine, almost as if she were playing a piano. A court clerk sat at a table near the judge's bench, sorting through papers. On the side of the room were thirteen jurors. Later, I learned one juror was an alternate, in case a juror got sick or had to be dismissed. Several feet from the clerk's desk were two tables, one for the prosecutor and the other for the defendant and his lawyer. The bailiff stood next to the big doors at the back of the courtroom, jingling his keys in his pocket.

The trial had already begun. The jury was seated and some legal *motions* were argued. The judge told the prosecutor to call the next witness. For the next couple hours, everything seemed similar to my youth court trial—except the attorneys *objected* a lot. I learned this trial was the fact-finding phase, to determine if the defendant was guilty, whereas my youth trial had been only for sentencing.

The defendant looked like he had been dressed up for the occasion—a haircut, fancy clothes, and even shiny shoes. There were several police officers in the room, but since they didn't give any testimony, I figured they were there to protect everyone.

The day dragged except for the part where the defendant testified. I don't think he made a good witness. His story sounded so fake that I knew he had to be lying. The hardest part of the day for me was listening to this one lady crying. She sat behind the gate on one of the long wooden pews. Since she was directly behind the defendant, I thought it was probably his mother. I decided that *every* mother cries, especially in court.

Finally, the judge banged the gavel and said that court was adjourned. He got up and left the room. The officers handcuffed the defendant and led him out a side door. Once the lawyers, jurors, and spectators left, the judge came back into the courtroom to talk to us. He explained the types of cases he hears and gave examples. And then he said if we don't make better choices, we'll wind up here. He sounded stern. But I wondered if he was like my dad—I hoped somewhere deep inside that tough shell was kindness and maybe even a desire to help someone.

During the ride back to the community center, I thought that if the reason for these field trips was to make me think about choices I make, then they were working. I decided I never want to be a defendant. I never want to go to a secured facility or jail. And if I were ever going to be in a courtroom again, it would be because I was a juror.

Saturday morning we worked near the school's main entrance. A girl and I worked on the flowerbed. As we worked, I listened to her talk about how much her mom liked to garden, and all about various flowers and plants. We pulled weeds and spread bark mulch around some big leaves that the girl said were called hosta.

When we finished, I walked to the sidewalk and looked at the entire schoolyard. There were a few spots that still needed help, but I didn't see even one piece of trash. I guess when you step back you can see the whole picture. It didn't look too bad. Actually, I thought it looked great.

That afternoon, Derek and I went to Mr. Barton's again. Since we had the basic shapes completed, Mr. Barton taught us more fancy woodcarving techniques, for more detail. After we finished that, Mr. Barton taught us how to sand the four-foot (1.2 meters) section. I rubbed the wood up and down in slow even strokes until it was as smooth as glass. Mr. Barton said we had one more class and then we'd be finished.

Mr. Larson dropped us off at the community center, and I saw my mom waiting for me across the street. On the way home, she stopped at a convenience store and asked me to buy a gallon of milk.

While I stood at the dairy section, Jeremy's older brother came into the store. He started a conversation, and I told him I was almost finished with my youth court sentence. He said Jeremy had gone through youth court for his first offense. After he finished that, he committed a second offense and was sentenced to probation. He was still on probation when we threw the rocks at the school window. Since he broke his probation, he's been staying at a detention center, waiting for a hearing. And because he was charged with a felony for stealing the skeleton, Jeremy didn't expect to be coming home for quite a while.

THE JUDGE'S ROLE

Judge Roosevelt Dorn, Los Angeles Juvenile Court, Thurgood Marshall Branch, insists juveniles under his control maintain school attendance, and he does not like his orders ignored. In Edward Humes' *No Matter How Loud I Shout*, Judge Dorn lectures a juvenile, saying, "You're stealing from yourself, no one else. . . . You're stealing your own future. If you keep on the way you're headed, you can only end up in one of two places: the cemetery, or the penitentiary. . . . I can send you to a place where you have to go to school every day, but I can't make you learn, son. You have to want to learn. I think the world of you, son. I love you. I'm sending you to camp to give you a chance to decide to help yourself. I love you."

A good juvenile court judge is expected to be a good dis-

Lady Justice is often portrayed as being blind. This means that a good judge is not influenced by things like socioeconomic levels, race, or gender. Her decisions should be fair and unbiased.

ciplinarian, to appear tough. Also, the judge is to show sincere concern for helping the juvenile and to treat the juvenile with respect, dignity, and understanding. For many juveniles, a stern lecture from the judge and some guidance from a probation officer appear to work. However, not all children benefit from such a confrontation. Many children return to the environment that caused their problems only to see the system as a joke because they run little risk of punishment.

ADULT COURT VERSUS JUVENILE COURT

Even the legal terms are different for these two courts, as these lists demonstrate:

Adult Court	Juvenile Court
guilty	admissions
cells	rooms
conviction	finding
correctional agency	Youth Commission or State Juvenile Correctional Division
crime	an act which, if committed by an adult, would be a crime
defendant	respondent
imprisoned	committed
jail	training school or camp
not guilty	denial
prosecutor	petitioner
sentencing	dispositional hearing
trial	hearing

Best Interests of the Child

Juvenile court is a little different than adult court. The judge must decide what is best for the child, not demand punishment for the crime.

The Right to Make Mistakes

In 1975, the press was not allowed in New York state family courts. The reason given was that children have a right to make mistakes and are entitled to protection from publicity that may damage them in the future. Today, these courts are still off limits to the press. However, if a journalist obtains permission from the judge hearing the case the journalist hopes to observe, the journalist may gain temporary admittance.

According to Judge Judy Sheindlin, records for both juveniles and adults should be treated the same. That includes fingerprinting, photographing, and sharing records between adult and juvenile courts. A person's record can be *expunged* (completely destroyed) or *sealed* (removed from

Residents in a juvenile detention facility often have the opportunity to use computers for both educational and recreational purposes.

When a juvenile is arrested, her picture will be taken in a room like this one, and her picture is added to her file.

the main file and secured in a separate file available only to the court) if the individual turns around his life.

LAW GUARDIANS' OPINION

Although many in court believe that kids manipulate their lawyers and the entire system, law guardians generally believe that their clients often have no idea of what their options are, or even how to present themselves in court.

MOTHERS

Once in a while, an unusual event occurs after a hearing: Still handcuffed, a respondent kissed his mother before being *remanded* to the juvenile center. Displays of family affection are rare in family court.

A VARIETY OF CASES

A juvenile court is responsible to hear and decide all cases and issues concerning children in its jurisdiction, including:

- Delinquency cases in which a juvenile is charged with an offense.
- Traffic cases in which the driver is a juvenile.
- Child support and paternity cases.
- Custody cases regarding with whom the juvenile should live or visit.

Juvenile courts also manage programs and facilities providing the care, custody, and rehabilitation of youth.

PEOPLE, PLACES, AND THINGS

- The *antechamber* is an outer room often used as a waiting room leading to the judge's chambers.
- The *bailiff* is the person who protects the courtroom, makes sure spectators are orderly, and carries out any special duties requested by the judge.
- The *bench* is the position or job of a judge in a court of law. Also, it is a long table on which someone can work.
- The judge's *chambers* is a room where a judge transacts business. Some people call it a judge's office.
- A *court clerk* is an officer of the court who is responsible for documents for each case.
- A *court reporter* is the person responsible for recording what everyone says during court proceedings. She is often called a stenographer. In some courtrooms, tape recorders are used in place of court reporters.
- A *gavel* is a small wooden hammer used by the person in charge of a meeting or trial to call for order or attention. It is also used to signal court is starting or stopping.
- A *stenograph* is a machine used by a court reporter to record legal proceedings. It is a mechanical form of shorthand.
- The *witness box* is an enclosure in which a witness sits or stands while testifying and giving evidence in court.

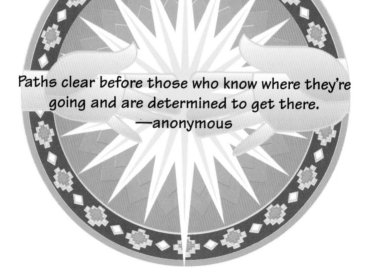

Paths clear before those who know where they're
going and are determined to get there.
—anonymous

8

HEADING TOWARD
THE FUTURE

"This is your last class requirement. It's a discussion on family re-lationships," Mr. Larson said.

He repeated a lot of what we had discussed in previous classes and went into detail about what makes a family. One girl talked about how she's living with her aunt and uncle. A boy shared how he lives with his mom and grandparents. Out of the eight of us in that class, only four of us live in a household with a mom and dad, and only two of us live with both our biological parents.

"What happens now that we're done?" Derek asked.

"You have one more session of community service on Saturday, and then you can complete your continuing education class. If any-one is interested, we have a class on Wednesday afternoons for any-one who wants to volunteer to participate as a youth court member. The class begins at four o'clock in the afternoon at the city court-house. You don't need to sign up now. You can just show up and sit through the first class without making any commitment."

Mr. Larson finished answering all our questions. As I walked out the door, Derek stopped me.

"Zeek, you gonna check out that youth court class?"

"Yeah, I was thinking of it," I said.

"I'll see you tomorrow."

The next day, my mom drove me to the town youth court. Even though my dad was not working, my mom had to take me since he still couldn't drive. His leg was improving with physical therapy, but it would be several more weeks before he'd be back to normal.

I felt weird going back to the new courthouse. It triggered the memory of the bad choice I made and the consequences of that decision. But when I saw Derek, I felt better. We waited in the hallway until we saw Mr. Larson.

"Hi, Zeek and Derek. I'm glad you came," Mr. Larson said.

"I'm not making any promises," I said.

Mr. Larson just smiled. "Follow me."

We entered a conference room and sat at a long table. Soon there were sixteen kids in the room. I recognized a few from my high school. Mr. Larson gave a brief overview and then he had us introduce ourselves. I could feel my heart begin to pound, and I wiped my sweaty hands on my jeans. *I don't want everyone knowing I was a defendant*, I thought.

"Just tell us your first name and what school you attend," Mr. Larson said. "Everyone comes in here with a clean slate, a fresh start."

I relaxed in my chair and didn't mumble when it was my turn to speak. We listened as Mr. Larson explained some general things about youth court. Even though I was familiar with some of the information, I learned some new stuff, too. Time passed quickly.

"We need to wrap this up because it's almost time for tonight's youth court," Mr. Larson said. "If you're interested in becoming a member of youth court, you need to fill out an application before you leave. Also, please take a booklet that explains terminology and the rules of youth court. There will be a total of twenty hours of instruction. At the end of the course, you must take a test. We call it our ***bar exam***. If you pass, you are eligible to participate as a member of youth court."

I reached over and took an application. I watched Derek do the same. I looked up and saw Mr. Larson smiling.

Saturday we finished our community service at the school.

"I'll fill out the appropriate paperwork showing you have completed your community service. I'll give a copy to Detective Smith, and you should receive your copy in the mail next week," Mr. Larson said.

He walked over to me and we shook hands. "Good job, Zeek. You're a hard worker."

"Thanks." His praise meant a lot. I don't think my dad has ever said anything like that to me. I tried to not seem too proud as I looked at the clean schoolyard, the flower bed, and the painted playground.

That afternoon, Mr. Larson drove us to Mr. Barton's house for our last lesson. We painted and varnished our woodcarvings.

"As you can see, you have each carved a four-foot walking stick. Some people call these canes," Mr. Barton said.

I knew what I wanted to do with my stick. I just didn't want to tell anyone in case everything didn't work out the way I hoped.

"Have you figured out why I like to start with saplings?" Mr. Barton asked.

"Is it to show us how you can take something that's crooked and make it useful?" Derek asked.

"Yes. And it's rewarding to see what can be made from a young tree. These walking sticks can be used for decorative purposes or to help someone who needs strength and balance. One of these can have an effect on people's lives for many years." Mr. Barton held one of our walking sticks in each of his hands. "You have done well. These are two of the finest walking sticks I've seen in a long time."

Mr. Larson patted my shoulder. "Don't doubt that you can do good because you made one bad choice," he said softly.

Mr. Barton told us we could call him any time we wanted to learn more about woodcarving. We thanked him and proudly carried our woodcarvings to the car.

Mr. Larson parked his car near the community center.

"Thank you for everything." I shook Mr. Larson's hand.

"You're welcome, Zeek. I'll see you Wednesday at youth court class."

"Hey, Derek," I said, "now that we've finished those rehab classes, I don't have anything to do Tuesday. Do you want to come over? Maybe we can shoot some hoops."

"Sure! I'll be there right after supper."

I told him my address. Then my new friend got in his parents' car and smiled as they drove away. I stood on the street corner, waiting for my ride. I looked at my handcarved walking stick, admiring the details of the black bass.

Mom asked me a ton of questions on the ride home. I think I talked the most I have in a long time. Her face seemed to shine, a little like that girl's did in the courtroom, the one who was going to be adopted. I was surprised I could make her look like that, but mostly, I just felt good not hearing her cry. We walked in the house, and my dad was sitting in the living room.

"Hey, Zeek, what's that?" he asked.

"It's a walking stick I carved." I handed my woodcarving to him, waiting for some insult or correction.

"Looks like you've got some skills with those hands after all." He handed the walking stick back to me.

I took a deep breath. "Dad, when you're ready to try something instead of those crutches, you can use this if want." I leaned the walking stick against the wall, and then I went into the kitchen.

"Can I help?" I asked my mom.

"No, thanks. Dinner will be ready soon."

I sat at the table and pulled the youth court booklet out of my pocket. *Maybe I'll be a lawyer*, I thought.

"Ezekiel, look." Mom pointed down the hallway.

Dad was coming toward the kitchen, his hand clasped around the carved black bass of my walking stick.

AN EXPERT IN THE JUVENILE JUSTICE SYSTEM

Macmillan Dictionary for Children (published in 1997 by Simon & Schuster) defines "expert" as, "A person who knows a great deal about some special thing." Jeffrey A. Butts may be considered an expert in the field of juvenile justice.

Jeffrey A. Butts, Ph.D., began his juvenile justice career in 1980 with the juvenile court in Eugene, Oregon, as a drug and alcohol counselor. Currently, he is the director of the Urban Institute's Program on Youth Justice in Washington, DC. He also holds the position of a senior research associate in the Justice Policy Center.

He has more than twenty years of experience related to at-risk children and youthful offenders. His research focuses on policies and programs related to the juvenile justice system. Currently, he is evaluating a national demonstration project to develop new ways of coordinating substance abuse services for youth involved in the juvenile justice system.

Dr. Butts has published numerous statistical and research articles in journals and magazines of the American Bar Association. His findings and policy views appear in many prominent newspapers and magazines. (Adapted from www.jbutts.com/index.htm)

JUVENILE COURT STATISTICS

The U.S. National Juvenile Court Data Archive currently contains over 15 million automated case records. The majority of the cases are delinquency and **status offense** records. Although information on each case varies, almost all records contain:

- demographic information (age at referral, gender, race, county of residence)
- the offense charged
- the date of referral
- the processing characteristics of the case (detention and manner of handling)
- the case disposition

The Archive's goal is to improve the juvenile justice system by collecting, documenting, and disbursing the information collected on youth processed through the nation's juvenile courts.

Computer technology is used to record criminal statistics and display evidence.

JUVENILE VERSUS ADULT SYSTEMS

Some Similarities

- The right to receive Miranda warnings.
- The right to an attorney.
- Pretrial detention facilities.
- Community treatment programs.

Some Differences

- The primary purpose for adults is to punish the guilty. The primary purpose for juveniles is protection and rehabilitation.
- Adult court procedures are open to the public and more formal. Juvenile court procedures are private and generally informal.
- Parents are very involved in the juvenile process but not in the adult process.
- Juveniles do not have a right to a jury trial.

At an adult trial, a lawyer interviews a witness while the jury listens.

A juvenile offender who never repeats his crimes is a success story.

SUCCESS STORY

In *No Matter How Loud I Shout,* Edward Humes tells the story of John S. who graduated from probation camp with honors and returned home to live with his parents. He now attends college and earns good grades. Although he is eighteen and legally an adult, he remains on juvenile probation. However, John never sees his probation officer, because the probation officer placed John in a low-risk pool of offenders who need not check in unless there's a problem. As far as the system can tell, there have been no problems. By definition, that is success in juvenile court.

CHOICES

Because it makes sense to them, juveniles will often choose not to be criminals if given another option. It's not that juvenile court has the power to change youth. What the system can accomplish is to give juveniles the time, opportunity, and tools to consider more constructive paths in life. This is a powerful lesson for the system and a reason to keep it alive.

JUVENILE AFTERCARE

Following release from an institution, the juvenile may be ordered to a period of parole or *aftercare* (care, treatment, help, or supervision). During that time, the court or the juvenile corrections department supervises the juvenile. If the juvenile does not follow the conditions of aftercare, he may be recommitted to a facility.

This sign in a juvenile detention facility focuses on the positive.

Residents at a minimum-security juvenile facility earn points for good behavior that can be exchanged for items from this "store."

Fingerprints are one way that police officers identify repeat offenders.

MAKING THE SAME MISTAKE TWICE

The recidivism rate for juveniles is 75 percent in New York State. This means that 75 percent of all juveniles who go to court will end up back in court because they committed another crime.

In the first six months of 1990, 11,493 juveniles were arrested in Los Angeles County for a first-time offense. For three years, researchers tracked these juveniles. At the end of 1993, the results showed:

- 57 percent went straight and were never heard from again. These were mostly ordinary kids who made one mistake.
- 27 percent got arrested one or two more times and then ended their criminal careers.
- 16 percent committed a total of four or more crimes and became **chronic** offenders.

How Does Juvenile Court Affect Recidivism?

Today, some juveniles are being tried in adult courts (depending on their crimes). In the United States, juvenile cases are more apt to be handled informally, out of court, than they are in Canada. However, once a juvenile case gets to court, U.S. juvenile courts are increasingly more apt to transfer the case to an adult criminal court; U.S. courts are 11 times more likely to transfer the case to criminal court than are Canadian courts.

A police officer's job is to apprehend criminals; the courts make the decision whether to try individuals as juveniles or as adults.

Cases Transferred from Juvenile Court to Criminal Court per 100,000 Juveniles Arrested		
	1986	1994
delinquency		
U.S.	28.94	44.36
Canada	4.66	3.90
property crimes		
U.S.	15.74	16.41
Canada	2.17	0.95
drugs		
U.S.	1.70	4.81
Canada	0.10	0.03
public order		
U.S.	2.43	3.72
Canada	0.70	0.38

According to several studies, though, kids do better when they are tried in a juvenile court rather than an adult one. One study, comparing New York and New Jersey juvenile offenders, shows that the rearrest rate for children sentenced in juvenile court was 29 percent lower than the rearrest rate for juveniles sentenced in the adult criminal court. A recent Florida study compared the recidivism rate of juveniles who were transferred to criminal court versus those who were kept in the juvenile system; the study concluded that juveniles who were transferred recidivated at a higher rate; the group that was transferred to adult court was also more likely to go on to commit felony offenses.

FURTHER READING

Ayers, William. *A Kind and Just Parent: The Children of Juvenile Court.* Boston: Beacon Press, 1997.

Humes, Edward. *No Matter How Loud I Shout: A Year in the Life of Juvenile Court.* New York: Simon & Schuster, 1996.

Hyde, Margaret O. *Juvenile Justice and Injustice.* New York: Franklin Watts, 1977.

Kuklin, Susan. *Trial: The Inside Story.* New York: Henry Holt, 2001.

McIntosh, Kenneth and McIntosh, Marsha. *Cheyenne.* Philadelphia: Mason Crest, 2003.

Murphy, Patrick T. *Our Kindly Parent . . . The State—The Juvenile Justice System and How It Works.* The Viking Press, New York, 1974.

Nunez, Sandra Joseph, and Trish Marx. *And Justice For All: The Legal Rights of Young People.* Brookfield, Conn.: Millbrook Press, 1997.

Pascoe, Elaine. *America's Courts on Trial: Questioning Our Legal System.* Brookfield, Conn.: Millbrook Press, 1997.

Reinharz, Peter. *Killer Kids, Bad Law: Tales of the Juvenile Court System.* New York: Barricade Books, 1996.

Rinehart, William A. *How to Clear Your Adult and Juvenile Criminal Records.* Port Townsend, Wash.: Loompanics Unlimited, 1997.

Sheindlin, Judy, with Josh Getlin. *Don't Pee on My Leg and Tell Me It's Raining: America's Toughest Family Court Judge Speaks Out.* New York: HarperCollins, 1996.

For More Information

American Sign Language Interpreting Resources
asl_interpreting.tripod.com/

Barron County Restorative Justice Programs, Inc.
www.bcrjp.org/teen_court.html

bridges4kids—Building Partnerships Between Families, Schools, and
Communities
www.bridges4kids.org/

Building Blocks for Youth
www.buildingblocksforyouth.org/index.html

California Coalition for Youth
www.calyouth.org

Easy Access to Juvenile Populations
ojjdp.ncjrs.org/ojstatbb/population/index.htm/

Hamilton County Juvenile Court
www.hamilton-co.org/juvenilecourt/

Justice for Kids & Youth
www.usdoj.gov/kidspage/

Juvenile Justice and Delinquency Prevention Act
www.dcjs.virginia.gov/juvenile/jjdp/index.cfm

Juvenile Mentoring Program (JUMP)
ojjdp.ncjrs.org/jump/oview.html

National Center for Juvenile Justice
www.ncjj.org

National Council of Juvenile and Family Court Judges
"Telling Our Stories from Juvenile Court" is an audio CD containing stories from America's juvenile courts.
www.ncjfcj.org/stories/

National Criminal Justice Reference Service
virlib.ncjrs.org/JuvenileJustice.asp

National Juvenile Court Data Archive
ojjdp.ncjrs.org/ojstatbb/njcda/

National Youth Court Center
www.youthcourt.net

New York State Unified Court System
www.courts.state.ny.us/

Office of Juvenile Justice and Delinquency Prevention
ojjdp.ncjrs.org

Southern Oregon Adolescent Program (S.O.A.P.)
www.soap.homestead.com/soap2.html

The International Child and Youth Care Network
www.cyc-net.org/index.html

U.S. Department of Health and Human Services
Family and Youth Services Bureau
www.acf.dhhs.gov/programs/fysb/switchboard.htm#

Publisher's Note:

The Web sites listed on these pages were active at the time of publication. The publisher is not responsible for Web sites that have changed their address or discontinued operation since the date of publication. The publisher will review and update the Web sites upon each reprint.

GLOSSARY

acquitted: Freed from a charge of a crime; declared not guilty.

adjourned: Ended.

antisocial: Hostile or harmful to society.

bailiffs: Court officers who protect the courtroom, make sure spectators are orderly, and carry out any special duties requested by the judge.

bar exam: An exam given in each state for admission as a lawyer.

behavioral: Deals with human action.

breathalyzer: A device used to determine the alcohol content of a breath sample.

chronic: Lasting a long time or happening again and again; done by habit.

compound: A fenced or walled-in area containing a group of buildings and especially residences.

crimes: Acts that are forbidden by the law.

curfew: A fixed time by which a person has to be indoors or at home.

custody: The care and keeping of a person or thing.

defense counsels: Lawyers representing the accused in legal proceedings.

detention: The act of holding in custody.

deter: To discourage from doing something.

disproportionate: Too small or too big for the circumstances.

diversion program: A program designed to change a juvenile's direction in life.

evidence: Proof of something.

felony: A serious crime for which the punishment may be more than one year.

first-time offender: Someone who has broken a law for the first time.

hearing: The opportunity to present a side of a case.

interrogate: To question.

juvenile court: A court that deals with juvenile offenders and children beyond parental control or in need of care.

juvenile delinquent: A young person or child who has committed an act that would be considered a crime if committed by an adult, or who cannot be controlled by his or her parents.

law guardian: A lawyer representing a respondent in a legal matter.

mentor: A trusted counselor or guide.

misdemeanor: A crime less serious than a felony.

motions: Applications made to a court or judge to get an order, ruling, or direction.

negligent: Not showing proper care or concern; careless.

objected: To oppose a statement or action.

offense: The act of breaking the law or a rule.

peer: A person who is the same as another in age, status, or ability; equal.

probation: A period of time for testing a person's behavior during which the person must report to a probation officer.

property offenses: Crimes against inanimate objects.

prosecutors: Lawyers who represent the government in court.

refers: Sends or directs to someone or something.

remanded: Returned to custody pending trial or for further detention.

respondent: A juvenile who answers in legal proceedings.

restitution: An act of returning something to its rightful owner, or giving money equal to the value of the object.

restrictions: Limitations on the use of something or on behavior.

status offense: An offense that applies only to children. For example, skipping school, running away, breaking curfew, and possession or use of alcohol.

truant: Absent from school without permission.

twelve steps: A self-help process that involves going through established steps to the accomplishment of a goal.

INDEX

Biographies

Donna Lange is a freelance author and editor. Her writing appears in magazines and several gift books. Her previous profession was court reporting, including juvenile court. She resides in upstate New York with her husband and three teenage children.

Dr. Lisa Albers is a developmental behavioral pediatrician at Children's Hospital Boston and Harvard Medical School, where her responsibilities include outpatient pediatric teaching and patient care in the Developmental Medicine Center. She currently is Director of the Adoption Program, Director of Fellowships in Developmental and Behavioral Pediatrics, and collaborates in a consultation program for community health centers. She is also the school consultant for the Walker School, a residential school for children in the state foster care system.

Dr. Carolyn Bridgemohan is an instructor in pediatrics at Harvard Medical School and is a board-certified developmental behavioral pediatrician on staff in the Developmental Medicine Center at Children's Hospital, Boston. Her clinical practice includes children and youth with autism, hearing impairment, developmental language disorders, global delays, mental retardation, and attention and learning disorders. Dr. Bridgemohan is coeditor of *Bright Futures Case Studies for Primary Care Clinicians: Child Development and Behavior*, a curriculum used nationwide in pediatric residency training programs.

Cindy Croft is the State Special Needs Director in Minnesota, coordinating Project EXCEPTIONAL MN, through Concordia University. Project EXCEPTIONAL MN is a state project that supports the inclusion of children in community settings through training, on-site consultation, and professional development. She also teaches as adjunct faculty for Concordia University, St. Paul, Minnesota. She has worked in the special needs arena for the past fifteen years.

Dr. Laurie Glader is a developmental pediatrician at Children's Hospital in Boston where she directs the Cerebral Palsy Program and is a staff pediatrician with the Coordinated Care Services, a program designed to meet the needs of children with special health care needs. Dr. Glader also teaches regularly at Harvard Medical School. Her work with public agencies includes New England SERVE, an organization that builds connections between state health departments, health care organizations, community providers, and families. She is also the staff physician at the Cotting School, a school specializing in the education of children with a wide range of special health care needs.

DATE DUE

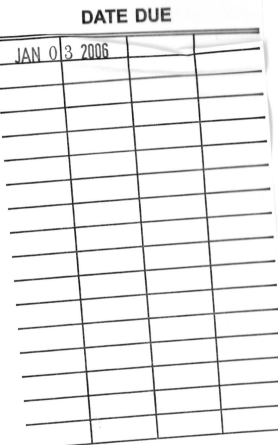

JAN 0 3 2006